The Chronicle of Abraham of Crete

(*Patmut'iwn* of Kat'oghikos Abraham Kretats'i)

Armenian Studies Series
Number 1

The Armenian Studies Series aims to make Armenian historical and literary texts available in English translations in order to provide a wider access to primary texts for scholars of Armenian, Iranian, Russian, Georgian, and Turkish Studies. Original monographs and proceedings of scholarly conferences focusing on Armenian history and literature in the modern period will also be included in this series.

General Editor
George Bournoutian (Iona College)

Advisory Council
Gia Aivazian (University of California, Los Angeles)
Aram Arkun (Zohrab Center, New York)
Stepan Astourian (University of California, Berkeley)
Houri Berberian (California State University, Long Beach)
Barlow Der Mugerdechian (California State University, Fresno)
Robert Hewsen (Rowan College, New Jersey)
Rubina Peroomian
Eliz Sanasarian (University of Southern California)
Abraham Terian (St. Nersess Seminary, New Rochelle, NY)

The Chronicle of Abraham of Crete

(*Patmut'iwn* of Kat'oghikos Abraham Kretats'i)

Annotated Translation from the Critical Text
with Introduction and Commentary
by

George A. Bournoutian

MAZDA PUBLISHERS
1999

Mazda Publishers
Academic Publishers Since 1980
P.O. Box 2603
Costa Mesa, California 92626 U.S.A.
www.mazdapub.com

Library of Congress Cataloging-in-Publication Data

Abraham, Kretats'i, Catholicos of Armenia, d. 1737.
[Patmut'iwn hamaṛot haṛaji zhamanakn Nadr Shahin. English]
The Chronicle of Abraham of Crete: Patmut'iwn of Kat'oghikos Abraham Kretats'i/ annonated translation from the critical text and commentary by George A. Bournoutian.
p. cm.—(Armenian Studies Series; No. 1)
Includes bibliographical references and index.

ISBN:1-56859-082-2
(cloth: alk. paper)

1. Armenia—History—1522-1800—sources. 2. Transcaucasia—History—Sources. 3. Nādir Shāh, Shah of Iran, 1688-1747. 4. Abraham, Kretats'i, Catholicos of Armenia, d. 1737. I. Bournoutian, George A.
II. Title. III. Series.
DS191.A2713 1998
956.6'2—dc21
98-32126
CIP

In Memoriam

Hakob D. P‘ap‘azyan

جامیست که عقل آفرین میزندش

صد بوسه ز مهر بر جبین میزندش

وین کوزه گر دهر چنین جام لطیف

میسازد و باز برزمین میزندش

Man is a bowl so finely made that Reason
Cannot but praise him with a hundred kisses;
Yet Time the Potter, who has made this perfect bowl
So well, proceeds to smash it to bits again

Omar Khayyam

Contents

Introduction	1
Annotated Text	11
Map: Geographical locations mentioned in the text	146-147
Commentary	149
Glossary of non-Armenian Terms	163
Selected Bibliography	173
Index	177

Introduction

The fifteen years between 1722 and 1736 were turbulent times for Iran and Transcaucasia. In March 1722 the rebellious Afghans reached Isfahan, the capital of Ṣafavid Iran, and laid siege to it. In May of that year, Peter the Great (1689-1725), urged by his former envoy to Iran, Artemii Volynskii, took advantage of instability in Iran and, having concluded peace with Sweden, moved his army towards the Caspian littoral. In October, Isfahan fell to the Afghans. Shah Solṭān Ḥosein (1694-1722) abdicated, while his son and heir, Ṭahmāsp [II], fled and sought support for the restoration of the dynasty.

By the end of the summer of 1723 the Russians had captured a large part of the Caspian coast and had negotiated a treaty with Ṭahmāsp. The treaty of September 1723, signed at St. Petersburg, gave Russia the southwestern and southern shores of the Caspian Sea (including Bākū and Darband). In exchange, Russia promised to assist Ṭahmāsp to pacify his country and to punish the rebels.

Although the treaty was never ratified, the Ottomans fearful of the Russian presence in Transcaucasia, the backdoor to eastern Anatolia, broke the 1639 agreement with Iran and invaded eastern Armenia and eastern Georgia in 1723. War between the Turks and the Russians was averted through the mediation of the French ambassador in Constantinople, which resulted in a treaty (June 1724) between the two that in effect partitioned Transcaucasia.[1] Ironically, historic eastern Armenia and eastern Georgia,

[1]The text of that treaty can be found in J. C. Hurewitz, *Diplomacy in the Near and Middle East: A Documentary Record, 1535-1914*, I (Princeton, 1956), 42-45.

populated mainly by Christians, were given to the Ottomans, while eastern Transcaucasia, populated mainly by Muslims, was awarded to Russia.

The Armenians and Georgians, who had been promised deliverance from Muslim rule by Peter, were thus abandoned and had to deal as well as they could with the Ottomans, the new masters of the region. The Ottomans took over Kakhet'i and K'art'li, Ganǰe, Erevan, Nakhichevan, half of Shirvan, parts of Karabagh, and a chunk of northwestern Iran. The mountainous regions of Karabagh and Zangezur, however, under the leadership of Dawit' Beg and a number of other Armenian chieftains, resisted the Turkish onslaught and remained, for the most part, autonomous.

In 1726, Ṭahmāsp recruited an able and ambitious commander, from the Afšār tribe, Nadr Qolī,[1] who had made a name for himself fighting Afghans and other rebels in northeastern Iran. Having rid himself of a rival commander, Nadr soon rose in the royal favor and was given the title of Ṭahmāsp Qolī ("slave of Ṭahmāsp" or more appropriately, "devoted to Ṭahmāsp"). After a number of campaigns Nadr defeated the Afghans and by the end of 1729 recaptured Isfahan. Ṭahmāsp was installed as shah and the dynasty was restored.

A year later, Nadr marched north to regain the provinces occupied by the Ottomans. Tabrīz was retaken in August. The Russians, who desired the Ottoman withdrawal from northern Iran and Transcaucasia, aided the Persians by loaning Russian artillery officers to Nadr, who proceeded to retake all of Azerbaijan. A revolt in Herāt forced Nadr to leave Azerbaijan and to march to northeasten Iran. Shah Ṭahmāsp, who feared and envied Nadr's successes, took advantage of his general's absence and marched against Nakhichevan and Erevan in 1731. The Ottomans routed his forces in Erevan and in January 1732 forced the shah to conclude an agreement that left Transcaucasia in Ottoman hands.

---

[1]The future Nāder Shah Afšār. Abraham refers to him as T'ahmaz Khan; Ṭahmāsp Qolī, the Khan, or *Valīne'mat* ("Lord of Beneficence").

In the meantime, Empress Anna of Russia (1730-1740), surprised at the heavy death toll of Russian troops from disease, withdrew them from the southern Caspian coast. By the Treaty of Rašt (February 1732),[1] Russia also agreed to withdraw her troops from eastern Transcaucasia, when the Turks were expelled from Armenia and Georgia.

Nadr took advantage of Shah Ṭahmāsp's humiliating defeat and his drinking and deposed him in the summer of 1732. The shah's infant son, 'Abbās III, was declared the new ruler, and Nadr was named regent. Nadr then renewed the war with the Ottomans. After some initial setbacks, the Persians, at the end of 1733, defeated the Turks and killed their general, Ṭopāl 'Osmān Pasha. The Russians, in the meantime, sent Prince Sergei Dmitrievich Golitsyn as envoy to Iran to assure the regent that Russia was prepared to aid in the expulsion of the Ottomans from Transcaucasia, after which they would completely withdraw from the region.

In 1734, Nadr marched on Transcaucasia. After taking Shemakhi, he campaigned in Daghestan. Later, with the aid of Russian artillery officers, he laid siege to Ganǰe. Confident that the Persians would repulse the Turks from Transcaucasia, Russia signed the Treaty of Ganǰe (March 1735) and soon after evacuated Bākū and Darband and returned to the pre-1722 boundary by the Terek River.

The Ottomans sent a large army under 'Abdullah Köprülü Pasha to face the Persians. Continuing to blockade Ganǰe, Nadr moved to intercept Timur Pasha, the Governor of Van, who was marching to bolster the defense of Tiflis.[2] Unable to block Timur Pasha, he marched on the fort of Kazançay. But the snow made his march impossible and he moved on Kars, via Lori. On 24 May 1734 he camped three miles from Kars. As 'Abdullah Pasha did not leave Kars, Nadr, realizing that provisions were scarce around Kars, moved to Aparan where he met the Armenian Kat'oghi-

---

[1]For the text of that treaty, see Hurewitz, *op. cit.*, I, 45-47.

[2]Present-day Tbilisi, capital of the Republic of Georgia.

kos[1] Abraham of Crete (Kretats'i).[2] He then proceeded to lay siege to Erevan and capture Bayazid. Leaving a force to continue the siege of Erevan, Nadr marched to Ējmiatsin,[3] visited the Holy See, and then moved on to Parakar.

It was here that he received the news that 'Abdullah Pasha and his army had crossed the Arpa Çay and was preparing for battle. Nadr rushed to meet the Turks and on the evening of 18 June his forces reached the vicinity of Zangi Çay, and camped on a hill. The Turkish army was camped in the field of Bağāvārd (Eghvard) a few miles away. The two armies fought the next day (19 June) and despite superiority in numbers, the Ottomans were routed and 'Abdullah Pasha was killed.

Turkish prisoners were dispatched to Ganǰe, Erevan, and Tiflis to announce the bad news and by mid July Ganǰe and Tiflis had surrendered to the Persians. Erevan held out, while the Persians laid siege to Kars and ravaged the country from Arpa Çay to Erzerum. The Ottomans asked for peace, and in exchange for Nadr's raising the siege of Kars, surrendered Erevan on 3 October. With Transcaucasia back in Persian hands, Nadr proceeded to subdue a number of tribes in Daghestan, who had cooperated with the Ottomans. By the end of 1735 Nadr had recovered (with the exception of Qandahar) all the territory of the former Ṣafavid Empire. He, therefore, issued orders to military commanders, governors, magistrates, religious leaders, and nobles, as well as to the Armenian Patriarch and other Armenian leaders, to assemble on the Moğān (Mughan) Steppe, where a *qurulta'i*, or a national council, was to be convened.

---

[1] Kat'oghikos (also transliterated as catholicos or katołikos) is a Supreme Patriarch of the Armenian Church. Although there were kat'oghikoi in Gandzasar (Karabagh/Qarābāğ), Aght'amar (Van), and Sis (Cilicia) during the eighteenth century, there was only one *Kat'oghikos of All Armenians*, and he resided in the Holy See of Ējmiatsin in eastern Armenia.

[2] Kat'oghikos from 24 November 1734 to 18 April 1737.

[3] The site of the Holy See of the Armenians.

Nadr arrived on the evening of 22 January 1736. By 3 February all the delegates had arrived. On the first day of *'Id ul-Fiṭr*[1](14 February) Nadr feigned humility and told the assembly that he wished to retire from service and that they should select one of the remaining Ṣafavids as their shah. Everyone knew that Nadr was not sincere and that he wished to occupy the throne. Fearing for their lives, they all begged him to accept the crown and after a few days of procrastination he agreed, provided they accepted a number of conditions. The Afšārs thus replaced the Ṣafavids.[2]

The coronation took place on 8 March 1736. The new shah having changed his name to Nāder, appointed his eldest son, Reżā Qolī, as his heir and governor of Ḵorāsān, and installed his own brother, Ebrāhīm, as governor of Azerbaijan with jurisdiction over Armenia, Georgia, and Daghestan. Several weeks after the Persian New Year (*nowrūz*),[3]Nāder and his army left the Moğān (14 April) and returned to Isfahan, from where he soon set out to retake Qandahār and invade India.

The *Chronicle*, published here for the first time in English, was written in the years 1736-1737 by the Chief Patriarch of the Armenian Church, Kat'oghikos Abraham III, who was born in the town of Kandia on the island of Crete. It covers events that occurred from April 1734 to November 1736. It details his sudden and unexpected election to the rank of kat'oghikos and his meetings with Nadr during the latter's campaigns in Transcaucasia. Abraham describes his presence at the *qurulta'i* in the Moğān Steppe, where he was an eyewitness to the election of Nadr as the new shah of Iran.

The *Chronicle* is among a handful of primary sources on the events that occurred in historic eastern Armenia and northwestern Iran during the years 1734-1736.[4]It not only paints a vivid picture

---

[1]A major Muslim holiday celebrating the end of *Ramadhan*.

[2]Ṭahmāsp II and his two sons, 'Abbās III and Esma'il, were later executed.

[3]The Persian New Year occurs on the first day of spring.

[4]The other Armenian source is Abraham of Erevan (Erewants'i), *Patmut'iwn paterzmats'n, 1721-1736 t'owi* (Venice [San Lazzaro], 1977). The most important sources in Persian are Moḥammad Kāẓem Marvī's history *Nāme-ye Tārīḵe*

of the socioeconomic and political conditions of the region, but supplies detailed information on the Persian army and administration not available in contemporary Persian sources. Furthermore, the *Chronicle* is a rich source of Persian, Turkish, and Arabic terms used in the first half of the eighteenth century.

The *Chronicle* was first published in 1796 in Calcutta.[1] That edition was based on a manuscript brought to India by an unknown person from Ējmiatsin (in then Persian Armenia). The next published version saw light in Vagharshapat/Ējmiatsin (in then Russian Armenia) in 1870.[2] In 1876 Brosset translated the Vagharshapat edition into French and included it in volume two of his *Collection d'Historiens Arméniens*, published in St. Petersburg.[3] In 1969 a Persian translation of chapters XXII-XLV of the Vagharshapat edition appeared in Tehran.[4]

It took another century, however, for a new edition to appear in Armenian. In 1970, a group of scholars at the Matenadaran Archives in Erevan, under the general editorship of Hakob P'ap'azyan, began to prepare a critical text of the *Chronicle*. Since a rough draft of chapters X-XXI was the only surviving part of the work in Abraham's own handwriting,[5] another manuscript which was complete and was judged to have been prepared under Abraham's su-

---

'ālam-ārā-ye Nāderī, 3 vols. (Moscow, 1960-1966), and Mīrzā Mahdī Khan Astarābādī, *Jahāngošāy-e Nāderī*, (Tehran, 1341/1962), see commentary.

[1] *Patmut'iwn Abrahamu Kat'oghikosi Kretats'woy.*

[2] *Abraham Kat'oghikosi Kretats'woy patmut'iwn ants'its'n iwrots' ev Nadr Shahin Parsits'*. The monastery of Ējmiatsin was located in the town of Vagharshapat (present-day city of Ējmiatsin).

[3] M. Brosset, "*Mon Histoire et celle de Nadir, Chah de Perse, par Abraham de Créte, Catholicos,*" II, pp. 259-330. The translation not only contains errors, especially in the interpretation of some of the Turkish and Persian words, but has condensed parts of the text.

[4] "*Montaḵabātī az yāddāšthāy-e Ābrāhām Katoğīkos ḵalīfe-ye 'aẓam-e arāmane,*" translation by 'A. Sepantā and S. Hānānyān, in the periodical *Vahid*, Tehran, 1347/1969. Professor N. Falsafī used parts of this translation in his article, "*Čegūne Nāder Qolī Nāder Šah šod*" in the periodical *Hur* (nos. 10-11, Tehran, 1351/1972).

[5] *Matenadaran Archives*, MS no. 7130.

pervision was used as the basic text.[1] Five other manuscripts, preserved at the Matenadaran, were examined in the preparation of the critical text. The first was copied after 1736,[2] the second was prepared in 1767 or later,[3] the third was copied sometime in the eighteenth century,[4] and the fourth was copied in 1797;[5] all are the works of anonymous scribes. The fifth was copied by Hovhannēs T'agvoryan in Constantinople in 1856.[6]

A number of manuscripts of the *Chronicle* outside Armenia were also examined. Two from Jerusalem: a 1775 copy transcribed in Erzerum, and a copy by Ter-Hovhannēs prepared in the Church of Surb Step'annos in Smyrna in 1821;[7] two from Vienna,[8] and a nineteenth-century copy stored at the Bibliothéque National in Paris.

The critical edition utilized the six manuscripts in Armenia[9] as well as the 1821 copy in Jerusalem and the two copies in Vienna.[10] The Vagharshapat edition was also examined. A Russian translation, prepared by N. K. Ghorghanyan, was included in the critical edition, which was published in 1973 by the Matenadaran Archives and the Academy of Sciences of Soviet Armenia in Erevan.[11]

---

[1]*Ibid.*, MS no. 1674 (The Vagharshapat edition used this MS as well).

[2]*Ibid.*, MS no. 5026, folios 159a-204b.

[3]*Ibid.*, MS no. 2616, folios 1a-72a.

[4]*Ibid.*, MS no. 5974, folios 86a-193a.

[5]*Ibid.*, MS no. 2722, folios 4a-36b.

[6]*Ibid.*, MS no. 2622, folios 220a-375a.

[7]*Archives of the Armenian Patriarchate in Jerusalem*, MSS. nos. 959, 699.

[8]*The Mekhitarist Library in Vienna*, MSS. nos. 616, 840.

[9]The *kondak*, or the brief summary, was taken from Matenadaran MS no. 1387, the only copy of the *Chronicle*, save the Vagharshapat edition, which contained this additional material.

[10]In the critical edition, Matenadaran MS no. 1674 is identified as *(a)*; MS 2722 as (*b)*; MS no. 2616 as (*c*); MS no. 2622 as (*d)*; MS no. 5026 as (*e*); and MS no. 5974 as (*f*). MS no. 699 (in Jerusalem) is identified as (*g*) and MSS. nos. 616, 840 (in Vienna) as (*v1*) and (*v2*).

[11]Abraham Kretats'i, *Patmut'iwn* (Erevan, 1973).

The present translation is from the critical edition. The French and Russian translations and the Vagharshapat edition were examined as well. Brosset's notes regarding dates are credited to him, while Ghorghanyan's notes regarding toponyms are incorporated in my more detailed annotations. Although some of the Turkish and Persian terms are explained in the critical text, many are explained here for the first time. Clarifications to the text are set in brackets, while variations of place and personal names are given in parentheses.

The majority of the more than one thousand notes in the critical edition, which explain the minute differences in spelling or the inclusion/exclusion of a particular word between the primary manuscript (*a*) and the other manuscripts (*b, c, d, e, f, g, v1*, *v2*), are not included here. They do not alter the meaning of the text or present additional information and are not helpful in a translation, which cannot be verbatim. They are useful only for those who wish to compare the various Armenian texts. However, those notes that identify the manuscript(s) that present different information, are included.

Abraham quotes several conversations in the Turkish dialect spoken at the time. They are written in Armenian characters. Since it is nearly impossible to reconstruct the original Turkish dialect (which is a combination of Ottoman and Azeri Turkish), the Armenian characters have been transliterated outright. An attempt has been made to render a few lines of Abraham's Turkish into modern orthography to demonstrate the flavor and style of that lost dialect. Although Abraham uses Armenian characters for the Persian panegyrics to Nāder, that material is available in the Persian primary sources and is thus transliterated from the original Persian.

The New Oxford Annotated Bible, *The New American Catholic Bible*, and *The Calendar of the Armenian Church* are used to render Abraham's biblical citations into English and to identify religious holidays.

Armenian terms have been transliterated according to a slightly modified version of the Library of Congress system. The same system (also modified) is used for Russian, Arabic, Turkish, Azeri, and Georgian names. The transliteration for Persian, with minor deviations, follows that of the *Encyclopædia Iranica*. Commonly used terms and anglicized forms, however, are retained (e.g., amir, shah, sultan, khan, melik, pasha, Azerbaijan, Daghestan, Eghvard, Erevan, Isfahan, Karabagh, Nakhichevan, Shemakhi, Shirvan, Julfa, and Tiflis).

The Armenian Church calendar, used by Abraham, is reckoned from the autumnal equinox of the year 552. It is, therefore, 551 years behind that of the West. In addition, in this period the Armenians followed the Julian calendar, which placed their dating system eleven days behind that of the Gregorian calendar. Except where indicated (new style, N.S.), all dates in the translated text retain the original Julian dates (old style, O.S.).

This work is dedicated to the late Professor Hakob P'ap'azyan (1919-1997), who served as my mentor during my IREX Fellowship in Armenia (1973-1974) and who introduced me to the collection of Persian manuscripts at the Matenadaran. His first gift to me was an autographed copy of the critical edition of this *Chronicle*, which had then just been published. He remained my mentor and friend during numerous subsequent visits to the Matenadaran. His work has shed much light on the so-called dark period (15-18th centuries) of Armenian history and has inspired me to conduct further research on this period.

I thank Dr. Abraham Terian for explaining the ecclesiastical terms and Armenian religious holidays. Dr. Robert Hewsen lent his expertise in the preparation of the map. Butler Library at Columbia University provided a number of hard-to-find volumes. Artemis Nazarian, as well as the AGBU Alex Manoogian Cultural Fund, helped fund part of the publication costs. My wife, Ani Atamian-Bournoutian, once again volunteered to read the various drafts of this study. I am, of course, responsible for any flaws that remain.

Iona College

A Brief History of Nāder Shah's Early [Reign] Composed by Our Patriarch Abraham of T'ek'irdagh[1]

[Chapter I]

According to the Holy Scriptures, that which God has predestined is inviolable. God does whatever He wishes. "Who has directed the Spirit of the Lord, or as His counselor has instructed Him?"[2]

[The Holy Scriptures also declare] that "The Lord makes poor and makes rich,"[3] and so forth. We humans are humble and naturally weak. Our knowledge is ridiculously inadequate and, as is stated [in the Scriptures], "We can hardly guess at what is on earth."[4]

Thus, some men who are born virtuous turn wicked, while others who are born vile become righteous. The worthy ones, however, are those who are born good and remain good. The all-loving God, the source of all goodness, supplied us with good will in [our] nature, even though some use [the gift of the Lord] inappropriately.

---

[1]The remainder of the chapter titles are in the first person. This chapter title was probably composed by the scribe of MS *a*. The title of manuscript *a* identifies Abraham with his post prior to becoming kat'oghikos, that of the Bishop of T'ek'irdagh (Rodosto, located on the Black Sea in Thrace). MSS. *c, e, f, g, v1* have the following title: *The Chronicle of the Story of My Arrival at Holy Ējmiatsin and the Death of the Most Holy Armenian Kat'oghikos, Abraham of Baghēsh—the Custodian of Taron—and on My Adventures and Suffering, and on the Appearance of T'ahmaz Khan in Ganǰe, in Kars, and in Ararat, and on the Battle with the Ottomans, Which Took place on the Plain of Eghvard and its Conclusion.* MS *d* reads *The Chronicle of Kat'oghikos Abraham of Crete*; MSS. *b* and *v2* have no title.

[2]*Isaiah*, 40.13.

[3]*Samuel*, I, 2.7.

[4]*The Wisdom of Solomon*, 9.16.

Thus, if [people] follow goodness, God, according to the testimony of the apostle, "will make all things work together for good."[1]

The yearning I had from childhood to visit the Holy See, the monasteries, and other holy places in the land of Armenia, was instilled in my unworthy self by God. At first, in the year 1168[2] [1719],[3] I was sent to Holy Jerusalem. I spent two years there.[4] [This occurred] during the time of the [feast of] the Restoration of the Universal Church of the Holy Resurrection and the Holy Places.[5] It was in my tenth year as the prelate (bishop) of the diocese of the city of T'rakia (Thrace).[6] The patriarch of Holy Jerusalem was the gentle-spirited Grigor;[7] the patriarch of Constantinople was the tireless theologian, Hovhannēs,[8] [both of whom were] students of Vardapet[9] Vardan of Baghēsh from the monastery of Amrdolu.[10]

---

[1] *Romans,* 8.28.

[2] The Armenian Church calendar is reckoned from the autumnal equinox of the year 552. It is, therefore, 551 years behind that of the West. In addition, in this period the Armenians followed the Julian calendar, which placed their dating system eleven days behind that of the Gregorian calendar. Except where indicated (new style, N.S.), all dates in the translated text retain the original Julian dates (old style, O.S.) used by Abraham.

[3] MS *c* has the date 1719 added by hand.

[4] According to a colophon written by Abraham, he stayed in Jerusalem from 1719 to 1721. The colophon is in MS no. 23 (*Harants' Vark'*) in the collection of the Armenian Patriarchate of Jerusalem, see *Grand Catalogue of St. James Manuscripts*, N. Bogharian ed., I (Jerusalem, 1966), 124.

[5] According to Brosset (II, 259-260), Abraham arrived during the feast of the Restoration (of the Church of the Resurrection), Εγχαίνια in Greek, which occurred in September. The Armenian Church Calendar or Typicon (*Tonats'oyts'*) of 1775 indicates the 13th of September as the day of "Dedication of the Holy Places at Jerusalem."

[6] Abraham served as the Prelate of Rodosto for some 25 years (1708-1734).

[7] Grigor of Shirvan [Shght'ayakir] (1715-1749).

[8] Hovhannēs [Kolot] of Baghēsh (1715-1741).

[9] A celibate cleric in the Armenian Church who has completed his studies at a seminary; a doctor of the Church.

[10] The Turkish variant of the Armenian word "Amlordvi." This was the name of the monastery of St. John the Baptist, for in Armenian it translates as "son of the barren woman." According to the New Testament the mother of John the

On 27[1] April 1183 [1734],[2] I left T'rakia and journeyed to Holy Ējmiatsin[3] [via] the sacred monastery of Glak[4] in Taron, the site of [the church of] St. Karapet, erected by our Illuminator, St. Gregory.[5] On the hundredth day, on Saturday August third, at the third hour of the day [after sunrise],[6] we reached the holy and all-sustaining refuge of Ējmiatsin.

Chapter II
On the Departure of My Fellow Travelers from Ējmiatsin to St. Karapet

Following our arrival at the Holy See, after we had kissed the threshold of the holy cathedral and had worshipped at the spot where [Jesus Christ] had descended, as well as at other holy places, we were taken to the supreme and holy leader, Kat'oghikos Abra-

---

Baptist had been barren before his birth. The monastery was located south of Baghēsh (Bitlis).

[1]MSS. *c*, *d*, *f*, *v1*, *v2* have 25 instead of 27.

[2]MSS. *c*, *e*, *v1* has 1735 inserted by another hand; MS *d* has no date.

[3]The site of the Holy See of the Armenians is the religious complex at Ējmiatsin (which translates as "where the Only Begotten descended"). The Persians and Turks called it Üç-Kilisa "Three Churches," which referred to the cathedral of Ējmiatsin and the two nearby churches of St. Hṛipsimē and St. Gayanē. The Holy See was located in the town of Vagharshapat (the present-day city of Ējmiatsin).

[4]Glakavank' also known as St. Karapet, is located in Western Armenia in the Mush Province. According to tradition, Gregory the Illuminator founded the monastery, which contained relics belonging to St. John the Baptist. St. Karapet ("the Forerunner") was, after Ējmiatsin, the holiest site in Armenia. It was also the ancestral burial place of the Armenian princely clan, the Mamikoneans. It was destroyed in the 1915 Armenian genocide and its ruins remain in Mush, present-day Turkey.

[5]Part of the historic Armenian Province of Turuberan, Taron was the feudal home of the Mamikonean clan. The center of Taron was the town of Mush.

[6]The hours of the day began with sunrise and hours of the night after sunset.

ham.[1] He was sitting in the garden in the center of a large veranda[2] and on seeing us he rejoiced and was rejuvenated. It was as if the great affection, which had been developed in my heart over the last twenty years, had suddenly burst into flame.[3] At the conclusion of our talk, which included questions regarding the condition of our brother, the Patriarch [of Constantinople],[4] the great city of Constantinople, its churches, princes, and priests, he [the patriarch] sent me to my cell.

I was directed to the chamber of the [late and] saintly Kat'oghikos Aghek'sandr (Alexander),[5] which was located inside the residence [of the kat'oghikos]. The bell for the Divine Liturgy was rung and we went to hear Mass. After that we sat for our meal. From then on, the kat'oghikos met with me on a daily basis and we talked in his room. Twenty days passed in this manner.

I then sought permission to return to the St. Karapet Monastery. The kat'oghikos, however, did not permit it, stating, "God Himself, seeing the weak state [of my health], has sent you to me. Therefore, at least for this year, I shall not let you go. Wait! Stay in the bosom of Our Mother, the luminous and Holy Ējmiatsin. Be my advisor and sympathize with my woes. I have known for some time that you feel close to me. My soul knows this. I have heard for many years, and [during my residence] at the Holy See, that you are [my] friend and are loyal to me and to those who hold my views." No matter how much I begged, there was no chance [of changing his mind]. He did not give me permission or [alter] his directive. But he did state "If God wishes, and with His help, I would like to visit Taron next year. Stay here with me and we shall journey together [to St. Karapet] and after you have made your pilgrimage there I shall send you to your diocese."

---

[1]Kat'oghikos Abraham II of Khoshab (1730-1734). He was also a student of Vardan of Baghēsh.

[2]The text has the Persian word *'eyvān.*

[3]The latter part of this chapter indicates that the two men had some contact prior to this meeting.

[4]Hovhannēs of Baghēsh.

[5]Kat'oghikos Aghek'sandr of Julfa (1706-1714).

I begged him to at least permit those who had accompanied me, Vardapet Harut'iwn, Father Hovhannēs,[1] the senior priest of T'ek'irdagh,[2] Father Hovnan, Father Pōghos, Father Gaspar of Boghazhisar and others from Istanbul and T'ek'irdagh,[3] some twenty altogether, to go on their pilgrimage to St. Karapet, and from there back to their own homes. We entrusted them to God and to Vardapet Hovhannēs, the prelate[4] of Kaghzovan.[5] He acted as their leader and guide and on Saturday,[6] 23 August, he took them via Kaghzovan [to their destination]. I promised them that I would follow at the end of the grape harvest. The blessed one [the kat'oghikos] laughed and said, "Fine, let it be so."

Chapter III

On Visiting the Monasteries Near Ējmiatsin and On the Reconsecration of the Altar of St. Karapet in Hovhannavank'[7]

The first Monday after the departure of my fellow travelers to the St. Karapet Monastery, 27 [25] August,[8] the kat'oghikos ordered his servants to prepare for a journey to visit [some] monasteries. He said, "I have not traveled anywhere for a long time and my

---

[1]MSS. *c, e, f, v1* do not include Father Hovhannēs.

[2]MS *g* reads, "Hovhannēs, vardapet of T'ek'irdagh, my student Harut'iwn."

[3]MSS. *a, d, v2* are missing "T'ek'idagh."

[4]MSS. *e, f, g, v1* are missing "prelate."

[5]Kagizman in Turkish. A town located on the bank of the Arax in the Province of Kars. In ancient times it was the center of the Armenian province of Arsharunik.

[6]Brosset contends that Abraham meant the eve of Saturday, that is Friday.

[7]The monastery of Hovhannavank' (Hohanavank' in the text) is located in the Ashtarak region in the village of the same name in present-day Armenia. According to tradition, its main church, another St. Karapet, was also founded by Gregory the Illuminator. Other parts of the monastery were completed in the 13th century. For more details see, *The Chronicle of Zak'aria of K'anak'eṛ* (critical edition, Moscow, 1969), pp. 231-245.

[8]The date is obviously incorrect since his companions had left on Saturday, 23 August, Brosset (II, 261) has 25 August.

heart is very heavy." He took me and more than ten Vardapets and we all left in good spirits.

At first [we went] to Hovhannavank', since the prior of the monastery, Vardapet Hakob, had come to Ējmiatsin and had invited His Holiness to consecrate anew the renovated altar and communion table on the northern side of the [St. Karapet] church built by our Illuminator, Gregory. The church possessed holy relics including some bones of St. John the Baptist. With great celebration we re-consecrated the altar.

Two or three days after savoring this spiritual and corporal happiness we went to the church of St. Sargis in Ushi.[1] While we were there, Hakobjan, the melik[2] of Erevan (Erewan),[3] who had been summoned by the kat'oghikos, arrived.

A horseman[4] arrived from Tiflis[5] the same day. He brought the news, as well as an official letter to inform us, that Isak Pasha,[6] had, without any reason, ordered the strangling of Ashkhal Bek,[7] the melik of our people [the Armenians] in Tiflis. He had kept his

---

[1]A village southeast of Mt. Aragats on the bank of a tributary of the Arax. A century later it was the center of the Sa'idli *mahal*. Today it is part of the Ashtarak region of Armenia.

[2]An Armenian petty prince, feudal lord, or secular leader.

[3]"Erewan" according to classical orthography, "Erevan" in modern orthography.

[4]The text has the *sayi*, from the Arabic *sa'is* (master of horse).

[5]Modern-day Tbilisi, capital of Georgia. It was at that time the main city of the Kingdom of K'art'li. It was ruled by the Georgian Bagratids until 1723 when it was occupied by the Ottomans who installed various puppet rulers. Nāder Shah put his own governors and in 1744 restored the Bagratids, who remained in charge until the Russian annexation in 1801. For more information see D. M. Lang, *The Last Years of the Georgian Monarchy, 1658-1832* (New York, 1957).

[6]Ishak Pasha was a Jaqeli Muslim from Samtskhe, who set himself up as prince in Tiflis from 1725 to 1728. The king of K'art'li, was Iese, brother of King Wakhtang VI. Iese, who had worked for the Persians as 'Alī Qolī Khan, now served Ishak Pasha and the Ottomans as Mustafa Pasha (1724-1728). After Iese's death in 1728, Ishak Pasha divided eastern Georgia into *pashaliks* (districts) and controlled the region until 1734.

[7]MS *b* has Azal Bek.

corpse hanging on the [city] gate until he received 50,000 *kuruş*,[1] after which he had permitted the body to be buried.

The next day, at my request, we went to P'arpi[2] and from there to Karbi,[3] where we spent the night at the residences of Paron[4] Khach'atur and Paron Ghazar. The next day we traveled to Mughni[5] to visit the Church of St. Gregory. Melik Hakobjan, who had accompanied us, was not feeling well and we stayed the night there. In the morning, after services, we went down to Oshakan.[6] The melik went to Erevan via Eghvard (Eghward),[7] but we stayed the night there. We left at dawn and arrived at Holy Ējmiatsin.

Chapter IV
On How I Once Again Visited a Monastery

Because of the love that the [kat'oghikos] had for me, the ill-fated one, he took me [with him] and as a diversion we went to visit large and small monasteries. We could not remain long in these holy cloisters, however, for [the kat'oghikos] was highly preoccupied with the affairs of and news from the Holy See. There were more than thirty[8] people in our party and just as many beasts of burden. Since His Holiness was an astute and thoughtful person regarding his subordinates, he did not wish to burden anyone else [with the problems at Ējmiatsin].

---

[1]Turkish small coin worth a *piastre*.

[2]A village in the Ashtarak region, birthplace of the fifth-century historian Ghazar of P'arpi.

[3]A large village in the Ashtarak region, which was a trade center.

[4]From the Latin *baron*, the term became synonymous with the Persian *āqā*. In more modern times it signified *mister (monsieur)*, that is, a respected and prosperous citizen.

[5]A village in the Ashtarak region.

[6]A large village in the Ashtarak region, the burial place of Mesrop Mashtots' the creator of the Armenian alphabet.

[7]The center of the Nairi region, it contains numerous medieval sites.

[8]MS *v1* has 96 people.

He, therefore, hastened to return to the Holy See, particularly since those were troubled times and His Holiness had been informed of the appearance of T'ahmaz Khan[1] and the advance of the Persian army. He [the kat'oghikos] rushed back to Ējmiatsin to care for its needs. We have become accustomed it seems from time immemorial to leave all of our problems to our leaders. We do not think or worry about anything but our own safety and comfort. The fact is that as long as one is alive one delegates all one's concerns to one's superior. It seems to me that [one does this] for one's own benefit and for [one's own] prosperity. But, after the death [of such a person], he is not remembered; instead of tears and lamentations, [he] is criticized and ridiculed. This is part of [the character of] our people; and the reasons are ignorance and ingratitude and nothing else.

I was once more commanded by His Holiness to proceed alone to the monastery of the Illuminator [Hovhannavank'] and to remain there for a week before returning to Ējmiatsin. When I had his leave to go, the prior of the monastery, Vardapet Hovhan, arrived on behalf of His Holiness. He took me to his monastery and after a week's stay I returned to the Holy See.

---

[1]The future Nāder Shah Afšār. The text has T'ahmaz Khan; here-in-after Ṭahmāsp Qolī Khan, the Khan, or *Valīne'mat* ("Lord of Beneficence")—depending on the Armenian text. Most sources agree that Nāder's original name was Nadr Qolī Beg. Shah Ṭahmāsp II, in reward for his services, gave him the name of Ṭahmāsp Qolī Khan ("the slave of Ṭahmāsp" or "devoted to Taḥmāsp"). After he deposed the shah and put the shah's young son ('Abbās III) on the throne, he took the various titles of *Valine'mat, Vālī-ye Mamālek-e Ḵorāsān* (Viceroy of the Regions of Ḵorāsān), *Farmān-ravāy-e 'Arṣe-ye Iran* (Ruler [Order-Giver] of the Land of Iran), *Nāyeb al-Salṭane* (Regent) and *Vakīl al-Dowle* (Lord Protector). According to Minorsky, after his coronation, he improved upon his original name by changing it from Nadr to Nāder ("wonderful," "uncommon," or "rare"), hence, Nāder Shah from 1736 until his murder in 1747.

Chapter V
On My Pilgrimage to Distant Monasteries in the Araratian Province

A few days later I was again ordered by the Patriarch to visit several distant monasteries in the Araratian province. His Holiness wished to visit these places himself, for he had not seen them [since] he had become the Supreme Patriarch, and did not wish me to go alone. Despite the fact that this Blessed Soul, wished, for a number of reasons, to go to these monasteries, troubled times and other concerns prevented him from leaving [the Holy See]. He, therefore, asked me to go.

Although ill, I departed the Holy See. I hoped that during my journey I would be cured from my painful fever. At first I went to Erevan, this was on 16 October [1734],[1] and I spent one night there. The next day I went to Holy Virap[2] and from there to Akoṛi[3] and to the spring of St. Hakob on Masis [Ararat].[4] Having concluded my pilgrimage there, I celebrated Mass, and after our prayers were completed we returned to the Akoṛi settlement.

After a short respite we returned to Virap. I descended into the pit, a necessary obligation for all devotees, and led a service [down there]. After ascending, I spent the night. In the morning, taking one of the monks as my guide, I went to Havuts' T'ar,[5] that is, the All Savior Monastery, where I spent two days. From there I trav-

---

[1]MS *g* has 18 instead of 16; MSS. *c, e, f, v1* do not have 16.

[2]Khor Virap or "Deep Pit," where according to tradition, King Trdat III imprisoned Gregory the Illuminator. A church, still standing on the Armeno-Turkish border, had been erected there.

[3]An old settlement on one of the slopes of Mt. Ararat in the Surmalu district (in present-day Turkey), not far from the town of Igdir. A strong earthquake destroyed the settlement on 1 July 1840.

[4]On a slope of Mt. Ararat, not far from Akoṛi, was the monastery of St. Hakob, which was famous for its spring.

[5]The monastery is near Gaṛni (present-day Abovyan district in Armenia). It was damaged in 1679 by the strong earthquake which also damaged the Hellenistic temple of Gaṛni and other structures in Erevan and on the Plain of Ararat.

eled to the monastery of Aghjots',[1] and after that to Holy Geghard,[2] where I stayed two nights. From there I journeyed to Gaṛni[3] where I spent one night. From there I went to Nork',[4] where I also spent one night. From Nork' I went to Erevan where I also passed one night.

I then traveled to Getargel.[5] The messengers of the kat'oghikos caught up with me here. He had two or three times sent men to seek me and to ask me to rush back to him. The first reason was that he missed me. The second was the arrival of the *nuirak* (legate) of T'ōkhat' (Tokat),[6] Vardapet Aghek'sandr, and Vardapet Sargis, a student of the patriarch [of Constantinople], later known as the overseer[7] of Kayseri (Caesarea).[8] The third was due to his illness. It seems the air that year was still and full of disease. The entire congregation at the Holy See was taken ill. The disease had

---

[1] A monastery near Gaṛni which was also damaged in the 1679 earthquake.

[2] A monastery located 25 miles from Erevan. It was also called Ayrivank' (Grotto Monastery). According to some sources, the monastery was constructed in the fourth century. From the thirteenth century onwards the monastery was called Geghard (Lance) because it was supposed to house the Holy Lance which was used to pierce Christ on the Cross. This fortified complex was also the ancestral seat of the Proshean clan.

[3] The settlement of Gaṛni, located some 15 miles from Erevan. It is a site of a fortress constructed in the third century B.C. A Hellenistic pagan temple was built there by Trdat I in the first century. Gaṛni is first mentioned by the Roman historian Tacitus. The Armenian historian, Moses of Khoren, also mentions it in his history. In medieval times, Garni was a town and a trading center.

[4] Nork' was a suburb of Erevan located on the side of a hill also called Nork'. It is part of the city of Erevan today.

[5] A monastery, currently in ruins, near the village of Dizak. Tradition has it that a small part of the Holy Lance was stored there. The cross-reliquary containing this fragment was blessed by Kat`oghikos Petros Getadardz (1019-1058/59) in 1022 at a tributary of the Chorokh River in Trebizond. Legend has it that the water began to flow backwards—hence the name Petros Getadardz (one who reversed the flow of the river).

[6] A city in Asia Minor.

[7] Armenian text has *dēt* (short for *veratesuch'*) which is the Greek έπισχόπος, or a custodian with a rank of a bishop.

[8] The capital of Cappadocia, now a city in Turkey.

spread and many in the village [of Vagharshapat] had died. Among them was Vardapet Sargis from T'ek'irdagh, Vardapet Zak'aria from Baghēsh, and a number of pilgrims. Awetis, a member of the Holy Council, other pilgrims, as well as many villagers [became sick]. Some patients were ill for a long time and were barely well by Easter [1735].[1]

After receiving the messengers and [after reading] the letter, I rushed back to Erevan and on 4 November[2] arrived at Ējmiatsin. Although I wished to visit Bjni,[3] Karenis,[4] and other monasteries, I cut my journey short, for the kat'oghikos had summoned me. I thus rushed to the Holy See to see His Holiness.

Chapter VI
On My Arrival at Ējmiatsin, the Illness of the Kat'oghikos, His Death and Burial

I arrived at Ējmiatsin on Monday, 4 November,[5] and found the kat'oghikos sick in bed. He had become ill two days before. During my visit I asked him the cause of the sickness and which part of his body was in pain. His Holiness responded, "My entire body aches. I do not know the cause of my fever."

Sad and confused, I tried to reassure and comfort him. [Thus passed] part of the night, until he told me three or four times, "Go and rest, you are weak and tired from your journey, you have just

---

[1] An unspecified epidemic killed the Supreme Patriarch, a number of clergymen, as well as some residents of Vagharshapat and Erevan. Abraham, as noted above, was also afflicted and although he survived, the fever, as indicated in the following pages of the text, would occasionally reappear.

[2] MS *d* does not contain 4.

[3] Bjni was the main center of the Pahlavuni clan and was a center of learning during the Middle Ages. Ruins of churches and a fortress are to be found in Bjni (in the present-day Hrazdan region of Armenia).

[4] Previous name of the village of Gumush, located on the bank of the Hrazdan (Zangī) River (present-day Hrazdan region of Armenia).

[5] MS *a* has 3 instead of 4.

arrived." Thinking that he would be distressed and unhappy if I did not leave him, I got up and went to my room.

Day and night, until Sunday, we were all in a state of anxiety and confusion. On Sunday we all quietly sat around his deathbed with grief-stricken faces and glanced worriedly at each other. We stayed there that night until the hour of four or five [after sunset]. The lay brothers told me, "Go to your room. Let him rest for a while. Your grief distresses him." I got up and went to my cell. My [spiritual] son, Vardapet Hovhannēs and Father Hakob stayed with His Holiness. They came to my cell after that night and said, "Go to His Holiness, he has a strange look and we are all worried."

I got up immediately, went to his side, and saw that he was near death. I begged him to bless us all and to grant us absolution. I sought his instructions regarding the Holy See, the members of the congregation, and his intimate companions. His Holiness speaking in a weak voice, or by moving his head [made it clear that he understood] my supplication.

Placing his right hand in my hands, he quietly and peacefully gave up his unblemished soul to the benevolent angel. It was like someone giving an apple from his bosom to another or to a beloved one. This occurred at nine or ten on the night of Monday, 11 November [1734].

At dawn we informed the Melik of Erevan, Paron Hakobjan, who sought the instructions of the governor of Erevan, the *defterdar*.[1] ʻAlī Pasha [the governor] was sick and bedridden. As they came to ask his permission to bury His Holiness, the governor passed away during the hour of the morning prayer. His Holiness had died in the night and the pasha died that morning in Erevan. The *kekhia* (*kadḵodā*)[2] [of Vagharshapat] had, therefore, to order the burial of the katʻoghikos.

---

[1]The title *defterdar*, in this context, refers to a commissary general of a province. The pasha was known as Defterdar ʻAlī Pasha.

[2]The *kadḵodā* was a respected and well-to-do elder of a community. He acted as the head of a village, quarter, or district.

Hajjī Ḥusein Pasha, of Terent, was named governor the next day. He had been the *mafaz*[1] [or] guardian of Erevan.

Melik Hakopjan arrived accompanied by one of the *ch'ukhatars* (*çukedar*)[2] of the pasha. On Tuesday, I, the unworthy, led the service and anointed [the kat'oghikos] with *meṛon* (holy chrism). We buried him in the Church of St. Gayanē.[3] I could not attend for I was stricken with fever and returned almost unconscious to bed.

The next day [Wednesday, 14 November], I, together with the entire congregation of the Holy See went to the Church of St. Gayanē and conducted a memorial service, after which we returned to the monastery.

After that they took five or six vardapets and me by force to Erevan. When we passed by the church where His Holiness was buried [St. Gayanē],[4] we saw many citizens of Erevan, Armenian men and women refugees who had fled [from there]. Seeing them we were filled with horror and felt helpless at their defenseless position. We wished to return to the monastery for we feared that the arrival of Persian troops would strand us in the Erevan fortress.[5] We begged the melik and the accompanying lackey, [who was] our former *mubāšīr*,[6] to let us leave. We thus reached Parakar[7] and rested for a while by a stream. I managed to gather five gold coins and gave them to him [lackey]. After much begging we finally got rid [of him] and returned to the monastery.

---

[1]Actually the Arabic *muḥafiz,* which translates as defender, guardian, commander, governor, or warden.

[2]This Turkish term (Persian *čoqehdar*) translates as "lackey."

[3]The Church of St. Gayanē was built in 630 by the order of Kat'oghikos Ezr of P'aṛazhnakert (630-641) on the site where, according to tradition, St. Gayanē was martyred. It is near the Cathedral of Ējmiatsin and is one of the three churches, which made up Üç-Kilisa.

[4]The text has the church of the deceased (*hanguts'eal*).

[5]See commentary for more details on the reaction of the population to a new war.

[6]Arabic term, also used in Persian (*mobāšer*), meaning manager, supervisor, inspector and in this case, superintendent.

[7]A village in the suburbs of the Ējmiatsin region, presently on the Erevan-Ējmiatsin highway.

Chapter VII
On How the Mubāšir returned [to Ējmiatsin] and Forcibly Took Me to Erevan

The next day, on Thursday [15 November], early in the morning, they took five or six vardapets and me by force to Erevan. Although I had an attack of the fever that day, I managed to get rid of it the same day. Since the *mubāšir* had arrived on Wednesday evening, we departed early morning Thursday. On the road, for various reasons, I shed many tears.

Upon arriving in Erevan they took us to the house of the head of the city. We were brought to the *ra'īs*,[1] or the *kadḵodā* of Erevan. At first he tried to persuade me, stating, "Since your *ḵalīfa* [caliph][2] is dead, and since you were close to him and loved by him, all the members of the congregation wish you to take his place. I shall inform the pasha that you are the new caliph."

I refused and told him that I was not suitable for such a position, especially since I was an outsider and a stranger.[3] I added, "I came to Ējmiatsin on a pilgrimage. I have the permission of the Sublime Porte and have official documents from the *kizlar-ağası*[4] and from *kapıcı-başı*,[5] Gül Aḥmet Ağa, granting me special protection. I request that you return me to my diocese." I spoke many others entreating words, the memory of which is tedious, but there was no way to get out of it.

Finally, he ceased his persuading and began speaking harshly. He sought to frighten me and even threatened me with death. I was confused and hesitant. He then left and went to the pasha. He re-

[1] The term *ra'īs* can be translated as chancellor, or chief magistrate.

[2] The Persians and Turks viewed the Armenian kat'oghikos as the caliph of the Armenian nation. Under the *millet* system, the leaders of the Armenian religious community (patriarch or kat'oghikos) were the secular chiefs of their nation as well.

[3] The terms in the text are the Arabic *ğarīb* (foreigner, alien) and the Armenian *otar* (stranger, outsider).

[4] Chief black eunuch of the Imperial harem.

[5] Chief gate-keeper.

turned immediately and stated, "You shall answer to the pasha!" He added, "Do not even think of refusing, for the pasha will kill you."

They then took me before the pasha [Hajjī Ḥusein], who addressed me in a severe manner and began to blame me [for the situation]. I responded that according to our old custom a *mahsar*[1] is formed throughout Isfahan and Istanbul, so that the inhabitants of these two cities can confer, elect, and confirm someone. Otherwise the Holy See and whoever becomes the kat'oghikos will face an unpleasant situation. In fact we have a number of decrees covered with many signatures and seals which place an anathema [on those who reverse this custom]. I told him much more, I shed tears and I grieved. But nothing helped.

He became incensed and said, "It will take more than a year for couriers to reach Isfahan and Istanbul and for the inhabitants of those cities to decide this affair and to elect someone. Troops are gathering on all sides and war is imminent. Ējmiatsin is on [their] route. By that time the monastery will be in ruins and its brotherhood, left without a leader, will disperse and no one will remain. Of what use will your election be then? I hereby order you: Agree and let them [the Church hierarchy] perform the ceremony and install you on the throne of the kat'oghikos according to your rites. Manage this cloister,[2] which not only belongs to you [the Armenians], but to our king [the Sultan] as well. We plan to remain here [in this region] and we need this place. I shall send someone with documents, petitions, and seals [to announce this to Constantinople and] to return with a decree[3] announcing your confirmation."

They took me by force and gave the following order: "Since you, the members of the Ējmiatsin brotherhood, have elected and wish that he become your leader, I have ordered that he become your caliph. Install him according to your customs and ceremonies

[1]The correct term is *maḥżar*, which is testimony attested by witnesses or a petition from the public.

[2]The text has *t'ēk'k'ē* a variation on *takya* (monastery).

[3]The text has *arzalam*, a corruption of *'arz 'alām,* which translates as "petition and proclamation announcement."

and obey him as you obeyed his predecessor. I myself shall provide whatever else you may need from the royal court; do not worry about it."

They, therefore, took me to the house of Melik Hakobjan. I spent three days there. Then they gathered the *kad̲kodās* of K'anak'eṛ, Erevan, and other places, the priors from [all] the monasteries, and, in addition, wrote to Karbi, Ashtarak, and other places to send their princes and *kad̲kodās*. They all gathered in Holy Ējmiatsin.

On the First Sunday of Advent, 24 November, upon the arrival of the superiors from various monasteries, they anointed me, the unworthy one, as the kat'oghikos.[1] They [thus] placed upon me the yoke of serving Holy Ējmiatsin and the Great Throne founded by our Holy Father, Gregory the Illuminator.[2] This occurred in the year of 1183 [1734] of our calendar.[3]

Chapter VIII

On How I Led the Brotherhood and Served the Holy See. On How the Persian Taḥmāsp Qolī Khan Laid Siege to Gĕnchē (Ganǰe), That is, Gandzak. The Arrival of Köpr[ü]lü-Oğli 'Abdullah Pasha and How He and His Army Wintered in Kars

After that I focused all my thoughts, strength, effort, and courage on the great cause of administering the Holy See, unfamiliar with the people, the brotherhood, the income and expenditures, the customs, as well as the complete lack of funds. The expenses of the monastery, however, were enormous and innumerable. I grieved and suffered greatly, but the Gracious Lord protected and aided. Sometimes we sold the fruits of the earth, other times we received

---

[1] He became Kat'oghikos Abraham III.

[2] According to an official bull, published in *Sion* (1877), Abraham appointed Vardapet Hovhannēs (whom he elevated to the rank of bishop) as his deputy immediately after the ceremony (1734).

[3] In MS *a* this sentence has been inserted by another hand.

donations from visitors, and at times we borrowed money. I have so far borrowed 20,000 *kuruş*.[1]

I, the unfortunate and tortured one, have thus managed the affairs of the Holy See.[2]

At this time Ganǰe[3] was under siege by the Persians. Köprülü Oğli[4] arrived with a large force from Amida[5] to Bayazid[6] and from there to Kars,[7] where they wintered. He ordered Temir [Timur] Pas-

---

[1]MS *e* has 1,000; MS *g* has 500.

[2]The leaders of Ējmiatsin, in the absence of a secular government, were, as noted, in charge of the Armenians of the Araratian region. They were also responsible for the financial burden and the collection of the taxes from the Armenian peasants who lived on the lands belonging to the Church. During the Turko-Persian wars and, later, Russo-Persian wars these peasants were not able to plant on time, their grain and animals were requisitioned, and some had fled the land. The Church, in order to keep its villages, had to borrow money at high interest rates. Rich Armenians and friendly Persian rulers would sometimes assist in reducing these debts. Corrupt or greedy local officials and inept or ambitious kat'oghikoi would, occasionally, drive the Holy See to the brink of bankruptcy, as well. One of the worst examples of such behavior occurred in the nineteenth century, during the reign of Kat'oghikoi Dawit', Daniēl, and Ep'rem (1801-1830), see G. Bournoutian, *The Khanate of Erevan Under Qajar Rule, 1795-1828* (Costa Mesa, 1992), pp. 77-85; and G. Bournoutian, *Russia and the Armenians of Transcaucasia: A Documentary Record, 1797-1889* (Costa Mesa, 1998), docs. 120, 121, 122, 124, 246, 258, 259, 260.

[3]The city of Ganǰe (later Elizavetpol', then Kirovabad, and presently, Gəncə in the Republic of Azerbaijan) was the center of the Province of Ganǰe, which at that time included parts of Karabagh.

[4]The Armenian text has K'oprlu, hereinafter "Köprülü." The Köprülü family held important positions, including that of Grand Vizier, in the Ottoman Empire.

[5]Present-day Diarbekir, in Turkey.

[6]The city of Bayazid (Bayazit, present-day Doğubayazit in Turkey near the Iranian border) was the frontier between Persia and the Ottoman Empire, near Mt. Ararat. The Armenian fortress of Daṛoynk' was located in that area.

[7]Kars (Qars) and its elevated fortress formed the frontier defenses of the Ottomans in eastern Anatolia. It is located at the westernmost part of historic eastern Armenia. The Persians had campaigned in that region during the Ṣafavid period. The Russians fought a number wars there in the 19th century. It became part of Russia in 1878 (Berlin Treaty) and became part of the first Armenian Republic in 1918. It was taken by the Turks in 1920 and is part of Turkey today.

ha[1] to take 10,000 *somar*[2] of wheat to Tiflis and to return to Kars. He also stored a large supply of wheat, barley, and other items in Kars, and dispatched war material to Erevan.

Chapter IX

On Ṭahmāsp Qolī Khan's Offensive on Kars via the Loṛi[3] and Kazakh[4] Provinces

In April, when the harsh winter conditions had ceased and the weather had become somewhat milder and we had entered the year 1184 (1735),[5] Ṭahmāsp Qolī Khan moved via Loṛi and Kazakh on Kars, even before the snow had melted in those mountainous regions. For we [later] heard from Persian soldiers and the Khan's retainers that they had planned to pass through a certain ravine, and that they had dug a road through the snow with their swords. They had begun their advance [through the ravine] when it snowed that night and closed the route, on which they had labored for two days. They then found a passage through another road and with great difficulty reached the border of the Kars province.

The armies faced each other and fought for one day. Each side had between 600 and 700 dead and wounded men.[6] The enemy turned and fled and the Khan returned to his camp, which was lo-

---

[1]Timur Pasha was the governor of Van.

[2]Each *somar* equaled 3 *puds* (each *pud* was 16.38 kgs. or approx. 36 lbs.). MS *a, b* have 1,000,000; MS *d* has 50,000 *somars*.

[3]Armenian Province in the northern part of eastern Armenia (border of Georgia). Remains of fortifications can still be found there (near the present-day town of Step'anavan).

[4]Kazakh lay between eastern Georgia, eastern Armenia and Ganǰe. It was populated with Armenian, Georgian, and Turkic peoples. After the Russian conquest it was part of the western Transcaucasian Guberniia, the Georgian-Imeret'ian Guberniia, the Tiflis Guberniia, and the Elizavetpol' Guberniia. Much of its territory became part of Soviet Azerbaijan and is in the present-day Azerbaijan Republic.

[5]In MS *a*, the words "and we entered the year 1184 (1735)" are inserted by another hand.

[6]MSS *c* and *e* have 2,000 men.

cated in Yakhni-Täppä.[1] Due to a lack of necessary provisions[2] for the troops and animals, this genius, this second Alexander[3] [Ṭahmāsp Qolī], returned to Ararat [so that] he could march via Bash-Aparan[4] on Erevan and Ējmiatsin.

Chapter X
On The Khan's Advance Toward Ararat and How I Traveled to Meet Him

On his return from Kars, the great Khan, moved, at an unhurried pace, toward Ararat. He arrived at a place called Shira-kala[5] in Aparan, and his army was deployed toward Karbi and Ashtarak. At this juncture our princes who were in the [Khan's] army, as well as *Kalāntar*[6] Melikjan prompted me, stating, "You must appear before the Khan with gifts and be willing to [serve him]." I departed immediately accompanied by five or six vardapets and with such gifts as [our means] afforded us. This occurred on Tuesday, 27 May, on the third day after the feast of Pentecost.[7] I reached Hovhannavank' that same day and on Wednesday I arrived at Aparan and proceeded to the place called Shira-kala. The Khan was informed of our arrival and he ordered 'Abd ol-Ḥasan Beg, the commander[8] of

---

[1]A fortified outpost not far from Kars.

[2]The text has the Persian term *k̠worāk*.

[3]A number of contemporary Persian sources praise Nāder's military tactics and refer to him as the second Alexander the Great.

[4]The center of the Aparan (Abaran) district during Persian rule. Presently the center of the Aparan district of Armenia.

[5]The former name of the village of Vardenut in the Aparan district.

[6]The *kalāntar* was an important city official. He performed the duties of mayor, coroner, and constable. The Armenians and Muslims had their own *kalāntars*.

[7]According to Brosset (II, 268), Easter was on 6 April 1735 and Pentecost was on 25 May.

[8]The text has *nasaqçı-başı*.

his guard, to receive us. We went to the camp and rested the night there as his guests.[1]

On Thursday, very early in the morning, when the Khan was ready to begin his advance, they [the guards] took the gifts and [led] me to him. I appeared before him and welcomed him. He said, "Welcome caliph! How are you? Are you well? Get on a horse, caliph, we are moving forward!"[2] Right then he mounted his horse and left with his entourage. His army followed him. He gave me soldiers from among his bodyguard and I followed them in the direction traversed by the Khan.

Chapter XI
On The Khan's Visit to Holy Ējmiatsin

When we reached the place [where his army had camped], the Khan went into his tent and summoned me into his presence. The servants rushed one after the other, [calling me] hurriedly and persistently, for they were accustomed in carrying out all their duties in a swift and urgent manner. They hastened me and conducted me to the Khan's tent. He invited me to his table to have a meal with him. I spent three days with the Khan among his troops until we reached the village of Doghs.[3]

The Khan then ordered me to return to Ējmiatsin. Thereupon I took the liberty to invite him to visit[4] the monastery and he promised he would. On Saturday 31 May[5] he stationed his troops on the plain, by the village of Hant[6] in the vicinity of K'ank'an

---

[1]The text has the Turkish *qonaq* (*konak* in modern Turkish)

[2]The text is written in Armenian characters: *Khosh geldin khalifay niji sēn. Chagh sēn. Dē at'lan khalifay kēdēk ilēri.* An approximate modern version would be as follows: *Hoş geldin halife. Nice sen. Çağ sen. De atlan halife, kedek ileri.*

[3]A village near Ējmiatsin.

[4]The text has the Arabic terms *tamāšā, zīyārat* (to behold and to visit a scared place) connected by the Armenian word *ew* (and).

[5]MSS *c, e, g, v1* do not have 31 May.

[6]Brosset (II, 269) has Hanan.

(Kiankian), a canal of the Arax River.[1] The horses [of his army] devoured and trampled down all the grain [of that village]. It was harvest time and there was nothing left to mow, for the [horses] had destroyed everything.

Waiting to receive news[2] from the Khan, I did not go to meet him on Sunday. On Monday I sent my co-adjutant[3] Vardapet Aghek'sandr to the camp to find out the wishes of the Khan. Vardapet Aghek'sandr returned at once. His face was grief-stricken, he was perplexed and appeared deathly pale.[4] Seeing him in that state I inquired the reason. [He responded] The Khan was incensed and had exclaimed, "Why didn't he [Abraham] come to meet me when I arrived here, to escort me to Ējmiatsin?"

I myself [was not aware of this] and the others were great fools, for they had not familiarized me with the Persian protocol and the customs of [that] land.

I was, therefore, seized with terror and despair. I said my farewells to all and asked for their forgiveness and prayers. I entered the sacred cathedral and prostrated myself at the spot of the Holy Descent. Groaning, wailing, and with bitter tears, I entrusted my soul to my Lord, God. Thus, stricken by terror, with a sinking heart and at death's door (*kisameṛ*), I arrived at the Khan's camp.

I expected torture and death, [when] the Khan asked, "Caliph, why were you not here to meet us when we arrived? And now you invite me to come to Üç-Kilisa?[5]

---

[1]According to Brosset the canal, after crossing Vagharshapt, emptied into a reservoir which was used by the Holy See. The Russian translation refers to it as an underground canal.

[2]The text has the Persian term *ḵabar*.

[3]The text has *at'oṛakal*, which can also be translated as "deputy."

[4]The text has the Armenian expression *kisameṛ* ("half-dead" or "almost dead").

[5]The text is in Turkish written in Armenian characters: *Khalifay nich'in o ch'agh k'i gēldêm san gēlmadên gharshulamaghay bizi, indi k'i ne ch'un t'aklif ēyladun Uch'k'ilisayē.* An approximate Turkish transliteration may be: *Halifa niçin o' çağ ki geldem san gelmaden karşilamak bizi indi ki nečün taklif eyledun.*

Shaking and tearful I answered, " My Khan, I am from Rum.[1] It is known that I am not familiar with the customs here. No one is to blame, but me. If you have to execute someone, execute me."[2]

[At my response] the Khan turned angrily to Mīrzā Mehti (Mahdī)[3] and said, "Why didn't you notify the caliph, for [he] is from a foreign land and does not know [our ways]?" At that moment the Benevolent God bent the Khan's heart to kindness and he became imbued with sympathy toward me, a foreigner, and said, "The caliph speaks honestly, he does not know the [custom of our] land. We shall, therefore, honor him with a *k̲al'at*.[4]

Right then, during my first audience with the Khan, he granted me a document confirming me as Patriarch and three other official decrees. The first dealt with the property of those whom Shah ['Abbās I] had driven out from their lands in the year of his campaign [in Armenia] and had taken with him [to Persia]. They had left [their property] in the care of Holy Ējmiatsin, other monasteries, and certain villages. The Ottomans, learning this, had seized these properties so that the owners could not reclaim them.

The second [decree] stated that those [Armenians] who had converted to Islam would lose their inheritance.

The third—No one could come to the monastery, without the Khan's permission, or oppress its inhabitants.

---

[1]The Persians called the Ottoman Empire by its former name "Rome (Arabic Rūm)," which referred to the Eastern Roman Empire or Byzantium.

[2]The text is in Turkish written in Armenian characters: *Khanēm, bēn Uṛumdēn gēlmishēm, k'i malum dur, bu ērn ēdēt'in bilmēm. K'imsann such'i yok'du, such' bēnumdur. Oldursan bēni oldur.* An approximate Turkish transliteration: *Khanım ben Urrumden gelmeşen. Ki ma'lum dur bu er adatin bilmen. Kimsan suçi yokdur, suç benumdur. Öldür san, beni öldür.*

[3]Refers to Mīrzā Moḥammad Mahdī Kowkabī Astarābādī, who was among the writers and caligraphers of the secretariat and became the chief secretary (*monšī al-mamlek*) of Nāder. On the day of Nāder's coronation, he was appointed the official court historian. He wrote a primary source on Nāder Shah known as *Tārīk̲e Nāderī* (see bibliography).

[4]*K̲al'at* (plural *k̲ila'*) is an honorific dress consisting of turban, robe, and girdle with which princes confer dignity upon subjects.

Immediately afterward the Khan ordered the *kal'at* which they put on me. It consisted of a velvet mantle embroidered with gold[1] and trimmed with fur.

Thus, though I had anticipated death I was granted the *kal'at*.

Let no one be amazed! Glory to the Miracle-Working God. You, Lord, accomplish amazing deeds and Your ways are inscrutable.

I then found my courage and said, "My Khan, if you so order, I shall depart and shall prepare the members of our brotherhood so that we can celebrate the presence of [my] Khan with proper festivities[2] and lead you to the monastery. He [the Khan] replied, "Good, let it be so." I immediately returned to the monastery.

Thus while they [the congregation] had expected to see me in my grave, they saw me alive and adorned with a *kal'at*.

All the members of the congregation were astonished, filled with rapture and praised God.

They rejoiced and proclaimed a great holiday.

They put on their chasubles, the young ones wearing surplices and with banners and candles in hand made a procession and went to him [the Khan]. Showing great respect, they escorted him to the Holy See.

Upon entering the holy cathedral, he paused in front of the location of the Holy Descent and asked, "What is this place? Why is the cupola here?" He asked about the holy images in the large cathedral, about its construction and those who had built it. We answered all his questions appropriately.

Putting an armchair and [spreading] a carpet in front of the main altar, I invited him to sit down. He sat and right away commanded the service to begin. The vespers commenced, for it was a Monday and the feast day of St. Hṛipsimē.[3] He sat, observed, and was pleased.

---

[1]The text has *ket'ipi zarbaf*, which should be *qaṭīfe-ye zarbāf* (a velvet or satin mantle embroidered with gold); *zarbaft* is another version.

[2]The text has *zinat*, which implies to decorate and to dress up.

[3]Brosset (II, 270) has fixed the date as Monday 2 June, following the Sunday of the Octave of Pentecost.

Afterwards the senior members of the brotherhood impelled me to leave the residence of the kat'oghikos, and in my vestments present myself before the Khan, following the evening prayer, stating, "Go to the Khan, thank him and bless him." I did so. For the Khan liked it when I spoke in the language of non-Armenians[1] [Turkish]. I did as they wished [kept answering his inquiries in Turkish].

He [the Khan] was pleased and at the conclusion of the prayers he sent through his *mīrzā*[2] 300 florins[3] as alms and departed. I accompanied him to the middle gate, where he sent me back, and went to his camp.

Chapter XII

On How the Khan Sent His Retinue to the Monastery and on His Departure to Parakar and Eghvard

That same night, before dawn, the Khan permitted his wives[4] and other family members[5] to come and visit the place of the Holy Descent. At dawn he came himself again. [Once] inside the church, the khan was happy and entertained his intimates by telling them all that he had heard about the place. After partaking of sherbets, rosewater and other sweets, and smoking [a water pipe], he came out of the church via the main door by the tomb.

He summoned me right away and thanking and reassuring me he stated, "Don't worry, don't be sad, and don't be scared, this house[6] is ours and you are a venerable old man. Your house will be

---

[1]The text has *aylazgeats'*.

[2]Mīrzā is the title of a senior administrative official or private secretary, in this case probably Mīrzā Mahdī.

[3]Large silver coin which equaled 1.5 silver rubles of the time. MSS. *c, e, f, g, v1* do not mention the 300 florins.

[4]The text has *ardzakeats'*, which translates as "wives separated from their husbands." Since this is not probable, they must have been part of his harem.

[5]MSS. *c, e, f, g, v1* "have family members", others have the term *uhik'* (which probably means the female members of his family).

[6]The text has *ocak* ('*ojāq*).

bountiful,"[1] (which means something like, "may you be healthy and may your house be plentiful").[2] "Since I have fed my horses and my troops with the [produce] of your fields and your stock, I shall compensate you in time [for your losses]."

He whipped his horse and rode off peacefully and contentedly to Parakar where he began to set up his camp.

I visited his camp in Parakar that same day bearing some small gifts. He once more reassured me and sent me back to the monastery. He then left for Erevan via Eghvard.

The Ottomans made a sortie from the Erevan fortress, engaged in a minor skirmish with [the Persians] and returned to the fortress. [The Persians] killed seven Turks and captured two prisoners. On Thursday, 5 June[3] the [Persian] army positioned itself by a hill near Eghvard. In the night when the Khan was still in Parakar, a messenger came and said, "The Ottoman general[4] ʿAbdullah Pasha has crossed the Akhur[e]an (Arpa Çay) River[5] with a great force and is coming to meet you. [He says that you should] be prepared to do battle, for this conflict cannot be resolved with words or by fleeing." The very shrewd Khan rewarded the messenger with *ḵalʿat* and said, "Thank God, I have been waiting for this for a long time."[6]

Chapter XIII

On How the Khan Sent the Prisoners and Heavy Military Equipment to Tabrīz via the Coast of the Geghama Sea

After that [the Khan] began to prepare for war. He removed all the heavy equipment, that is, the large tents, [as well as] the prisoners,

---

[1]The text has *avadan* a derivative of *ābādān.*

[2]The explanation in parentheses appears in the text.

[3]June 5 does not appear in MSS. *c, e, f, v1*.

[4]The text has *saraskar*, that is *sarʿaskar* (head of army).

[5]The Arpa Çay (Akhuryan in modern Armenian orthography) acted as an unofficial boundary between the Ottoman and Persian Empires. Today it forms the border between Armenia and Turkey.

[6]The context suggests that an Ottoman courier brought the message.

those who were no use [in war], who could not fight, and the women and sent them via the coastal [road] by the Geghama[1] Sea to Tabrīz.

He stayed with 18,000 Aryan[2] troops and [positioned] his army and [his] tent on a high hill, which was known from olden days as Akhi-Täppä (Aq-Tappe). He pitched his tent there and ordered the building of fortifications in the form of towers that resembled half-circular blocks around the hill. The height of the fortifications, which resembled bastion ramparts, equaled two *gaz*[3]--foreigners call [these fortifications] *matariz*[4]--so that if the Ottomans attacked suddenly, one could bombard them with cannons or use other instruments of war. In this fashion, the Khan erected three or four rows of these bastions around the hill.

On Saturday, Köprülü-Oğli appeared with his army from the upper side of Aparan. He descended to the foot of Mt. Ara[5] opposite Eghvard. Facing each other the *charkhach*[6] collided. Each side lost several men and they disengaged.

The Persians labored all night to resolve the water shortage. They slaughtered all their sheep and goats, skinned them, and filled the skins with water. They also filled other vessels on the hill with

---

[1]Lake Sevan, a large body of water located in the highlands northeast of Erevan.

[2]Abraham uses the term "Aryan" to distinguish the Persians from the Ottoman Turks. In reality, most of the Khan's army was composed of various Turkish tribes. Persians, Kurds, Afghans, Georgians, and Armenians formed a small part of his army. The text also indicates that Nāder used Turkish when he spoke with Abraham and his [Nāder's] subordinates.

[3]A Persian measure equal to half the height of a man of ordinary stature, or 24 finger-breadths, or six hands, or a yard when measuring cloth, or a cubit.

[4]The term is the plural of *matars* or *matrez* (bastion, wooden or earthen parapet, palisade, or shield).

[5]Mt. Ara is situated near Karbi between Alagöz and Eçek Meydān.

[6]The correct term is *čarke̱čī* meaning an advance detachment of light troops, that is, skirmishers in front of the main body of the army.

water as well, for the Zangi (Hrazdan) River[1] lay two days march behind them, while the Turkish army was in front of them.[2]

Chapter XIV

On The Battle on the Plain of Eghvard and the Crushing Defeat of the Ottomans by the Persians

Great are the acts of God and deeply concealed in the mind of the Almighty. Who among mortals can discover or comprehend them?[3] My mind is now delighted and amazed at the wonder of God and the fairness of the Creator.

For on this same field, fifteen years ago,[4] three Turkish detachments, of 300 men [each], killed 12,000 Persians.[5] Their bloody corpses were scattered throughout the plain and became food for beasts and birds of prey. The exact same revenge was accorded to them [the Persians] by the Almighty.

After Saturday, on Sunday 8 June,[6] from two o'clock in the afternoon the battle commenced.

The great Khan, the shrewd Ṭahmāsp-Qolī, during the [early stages] of the battle, revealed a part of his army, as if [he had] only three detachments of 1,000 men [each]. Seeing so few soldiers, the Ottomans did not take the Persian army seriously. They immedi-

---

[1]The Zangi Çay flows from the north to Erevan. Eghvard is along the route of the river between Erevan and Karbi, see map.

[2]The Ottomans camped at the foot of Mt. Ara near the plain of Eghvard. According to Mīrzā Mahdī, two *parasangs* (several miles) separated the two armies, *op. cit.*, p. 252.

[3]Refers to *Psalms* 92.5-6 "How great are your works, O Lord! Your thoughts are very deep! The dullard cannot know, the stupid cannot understand this."

[4]This is an obvious error, for the only Turkish campaigns in the Ararat region during the early part of the eighteenth century occurred in 1724, which was eleven and not fifteen years prior to the battle of Eghvard, and in 1731 (four years before Eghvard).

[5]MSS. *c, e, f, v1* have 15,000 instead of 12,000.

[6]MSS. *c, e, f, v1* do not have 8 June.

ately ordered their troops to horse, with the Janissaries marching on foot ahead and the cannons in the back.

According to some, the Turks had sixty[1] cannons, but I saw only forty.

Behind the cannons there was a formation of knights and among them was the commander, ʻAbdullah Pasha, with Saru Mustafa Pasha [a son-in-law of the Sultan],[2] Timur [Pasha of Van], Pʻolad,[3] and Kör-Çavuş, who during the night had boasted, "Where can the Persians hide from my cavalry, which will trample them?"

When they began the fight, the Turks were fooled by the small numbers of Persians and moved away from the foot of Mt. Ara. They attacked the Persians, who fled and who dragged the Turks even further from [the foot of Mt. Ara] and into the plain of Eghvard.[4] Accordingly the 18,000-strong Persian army[5] came out of the ravine, from the direction of Erevan [from the South]. Despite their large numbers, which were grouped in regiments, they did not attack for they did not have the Khan's permission. Only the three detachments of 1,000 men each, which the Khan had sent [earlier] engaged in battle.

---

[1] Sixty is absent from MS *g*.

[2] He was also the governor of Diarbekir.

[3] Pulad Pasha, the former governor of Hamadān.

[4] Mīrzā Mahdī calls it Bāğāvard, also known as Morād Tappe, *op. cit.*, pp. 252, 255. All the non-Armenian sources refer to the site as Bāğāvard. The Armenians, however, continued to use the original name of the settlement, which was referred to as Eghward from medieval times.

[5] Although Mīrzā Mahdī gives the number of troops as 15,000, *Ibid.* p. 252; both he and Abraham must be referring to the advance guard. Moḥammad Kāẓem has 15,000 as well, but refers to them as the core group around Nāder, rather than the entire army, *op. cit.* I, 394. Hanway records 55,000 which seems more accurate, J. Hanway, *An Historical Account etc.*...IV (London, 1753), 119. Hammer in his monumental *History of the Ottoman Empire*, XIV (Paris, 1835-1843), 336, mentions 80,000 Ottomans and 71,000 Persians. Mīrzā Mahdī puts the number of Ottomans as 70,000 cavalry and 50,000 infantry, which seems too high, *op. cit.*, p. 252; while Moḥammad Kāżem has the totally inflated figure of 300,000, *op. cit.*, I, 393.

The Khan, according to his Aryan habit,[1] positioned the [troops], stationed and dispatched [them], firing his field guns to the right, left, and center. He also used falconets,[2] that is, large firearms mounted on the saddles of some 700 camels.[3] He ordered to fire the large cannons first and then use the falconets.

The armies faced each other and the infantry struck with weapons from both sides. Thus on 8 June (19 June N.S.),[4] on a Sunday, from three to five in the afternoon, fire and guns filled the battlefield. The Turks succeeded in firing only two or three volleys of cannon, while the Persians fired some 300 or probably more cannon balls. They [the Persians] also fired many shots from falconets and muskets.

The Khan suddenly rushed the Ottoman artillery and captured it. When the Ottomans saw and heard [from others] that the Persians had captured their guns, they immediately turned and fled. The Persians chased [after them] and slaughtered them. Killing [some] they drove others to the upper side of Mt. Ara, opposite Saghmosavank'.[5] Yet others were [chased] to the lower side, toward Ashtarak,[6] while those in the middle were pushed toward the

---

[1]Once again, the term *Aryan* is used to distinguish the Persians from the Turks and to present the Khan in a more favorable light to Armenian readers. In reality Nāder was from a Türkmen tribe (the Afšār).

[2]The falconets were light cannon used in battle. These were swivel-type known as *zamburak* (the text has *zambarak*) mounted on camels

[3]MSS. *e, f, v1* have 500 instead of 700.

[4]June 18 and 19 has been suggested as the exact day of the battle. Mīrzā Mahdī, *Jahāngošāy-e Nāderī*, p. 254 gives the date of the battle as 26 *Muḥarram,* 1148 A. H. (June 18). Nader's letter to the Russian envoy Golitsyn and other Russian and English reports confirm Abraham's date of June 19, see L. Lockhart, *Nadir Shah* (London, 1938), p. 88 n. 4. Hammer relying on a letter (dated June 20) from the Italian P. Nicolo de Girgenti, the Capuchin prefect in Georgia (Akhaltsikhe), mistakenly places the battle on June 14, that is 22 *Muharram*, *op. cit.*, XIV, 337.

[5]Located in the Ashtarak region on the bank of the Kazakh River, between Mt. Aragats and Mt. Ara. According to tradition, Gregory the Illuminator founded it.

[6]Abraham strangely does not mention the role of the Armenians in this battle. According to Mīrzā Mahdī, the Armenians of Ashtarak cut off several thou-

Kars River, opposite Hovhannavank‘, Karbi, and Mughni. It seems more fell into the gorge of the Kars [River] than died by the sword.

The [Persians] also constrained the [Turkish] commander, Köprülü-Oğli. He tried to descend through the stony bank of the gorge, through a narrow and rocky path, but could not keep his mount. He fell from his horse, received a severe head wound, and was close to death. A certain lowly Persian cut off his head and took it to the Khan. When the Turkish prisoners of war informed him [the Khan], that it was indeed the head of General ‘Abdullah Pasha, he immediately ordered that *ḵal‘at* be given to the one who had brought the head. He also promised *ḵal‘at* to those who would bring him the body. They immediately found [the body of ‘Abdullah Pasha] and presented it. The Khan ordered that [the body] be taken to Karbi, [where] they performed the rites, put it [the body] in a coffin, delivered it to Kars, where it was buried.

During the battle, Damad[1]Mustafa Pasha was also killed. The Khan ordered that his body be found as well. It was taken to Erevan, where after performing the necessary rite, it was buried in the new mosque.

We were also told that two other pashas, with the rank of senior captain, were also killed during the battle, the first an Albanian, the second a Bosnian.

The Persians won a great victory seizing [the territory] bordering from the Akhurean, that is Arpa Çay, in the north to the foot of Mt. Aragats in the south stretching to he same river.

Following the battle, the Khan ordered that the casualties be counted. It was discovered that 40,000[2]Ottomans had been killed, while no more than fifteen or twenty[3]Persians had died. The Ottomans were so benumbed before the Persians that they could not

---

sand fleeing Ottomans and held off their escape with stones and clubs until the Ottomans were killed by the pursuing Persians, *op. cit.*, p. 255. See commentary.

[1]*Damad* means son-in-law.

[2]Mīrzā Mahdī has 50,000, p. 254

[3]MS *g* does not have the number twenty. Such a low count is improbable. Mīrzā Mahdī does not give the number of Persian casualties.

even lift a finger of a hand to defend themselves against their killers.[1]

Chapter XV
How I Visited the Great Khan, Traveling among Corpses

After three days, on Tuesday, I, the unworthy Abraham, the spiritual patriarch, went to visit the Khan in the direction of Eghvard, near the hill known as Murad-Täppä. On the road, beginning from Ashtarak to the plain of Eghvard I came upon countless bodies. Some were still alive and the Persians were searching them and killing them. I saw this with my own eyes during my journey.

I accidentally came upon a nearly dead Armenian, whom the Persians wanted to kill. I rescued him from them, put him on a mule and instructed my footman,[2] Pōghos, to accompany him to Ashtarak and to house him in a cell of the church. I ordered that the monks show concern and take care of him. He recovered and became a *katēpan*, that is a gardener, and remained there in someone's service.

Many wounded--Albanians, Turks, Armenians, and Greeks[3]--who survived the battle, arrived in Ējmiatsin the day after [the battle]. I ordered many of them to be cared for. We send the Turks to Erevan during the night. Some of the Armenians and Greeks died, but others left to wherever they wished.

---

[1]MS *a* has the following extra line: This occurred in 1184.

[2]The text has *šāṭer*.

[3]It is interesting to note that the Ottoman army had non-Muslims among its troops, see commentary.

Chapter XVI
On How the Khan and His Army Ascended the Highlands in the Vicinity of Holy Geghard and Goradara and How Two Months Later He Descended and Advanced toward Kars

Afterwards the Khan climbed to the top of the mountains near Ghrkhbulakh (Kırk-Bulağ),[1] in the vicinity of Geghard and Goradara. His army, now scattered, camped [in the expanse] up to Tsaghkunadzor (Tsaghknaydzor)[2] and the coast of Sea of Geghama. The army stayed there and rested until the end of July, and in the beginning of August it began to descend, by the same route it had ascended, and reached the battlefield, to the hill called Mubārak-Täppä. The hill was previously called Akhi-Täppä, but since the Khan was victorious in the battle, the hill was renamed Mubārak-Täppä and it has remained so.

When the most fortunate Khan reached that hill, I was with him, for he had requested my presence. In the morning when [the Khan] wanted to begin his march, he ascended that hill and summoned me and the grandees: khans, *mīrzās*, the *kalāntar* and the melik were also [summoned] to the top of the hill, to the spot where he had pitched his tent during the victorious battle.

He spoke with us for a long time. First, about the dome, in the shape of his tent, which he planned to erect there for posterity in memory of his victory. Second [about how] we should prepare and defend ourselves against the treachery and hostility of the people living next to our borders.

He continued to speak for a full hour, either with the khans or with me, until we descended from the hill onto the plain. He then ordered us to mount our horses and follow him. He spent that night in a place called Bash-Aparan and invited me to dinner that evening.

---

[1] The village of Akunk in the Abovyan district. The name derives from the Turkish for "forty-springs" (Kırk-Bulağ).

[2] In the Hrazdan region today where the Kecharis architectural complex is located.

In the morning he sent Bābā Khan, Sardār Khan, the Khan of Erevan, and the Khan of Naḵǰevān (Nakhichevan) to their domains. Erevan was under siege at the time and he wanted to make sure that the khans surrounded it from four sides and guarded against anyone leaving or entering it.

He took me, however, to a place called Chinli (J̌inli) and once again invited me to his table. Since it was the Fast for the Assumption of the Virgin, I gathered courage and said, " My Khan, You have already invited me five or six times to your table. Each time it occurred during a fasting day. Since I thirst for the sweetness of your food, which to me resembles manna from heaven, I beg your highness to permit me, as one who prays for you, to take to my quarters the food which is in front of me." [The Khan] laughed happily and said, "Caliph, will you eat tomorrow?" "No," I replied. This touched him and he said, "Fine, tomorrow you shall also travel with me. You are once again invited to my table, for I have eaten much of your bread. After that I shall permit you to return to Üç-Kilisa."

I thus traveled with him the next day as well. That night he again invited me [to supper]. Ordering [the servants] to fill a plate with pilaf, which was in front of him, the Khan commanded his servants to keep it and to take it to my tent. It was done as he had wished.

After we ate—they, that which was forbidden [to me] during the fast, and I, honey and sweets—the meal was over. We washed our hands. I got up, thanked [the Khan] and remained standing. He said, "Caliph, I allow you to depart.[1] Have a good journey! Go to your monastery and pray for us."

I begged him to permit me to travel with him until the Arpa Çay, but the second Alexander was totally against it. He did not permit it and said the following: "You are old, we take pity on you. Go, return to your house and pray for us."

---

[1]The text has *moraḵḵaṣ* (to leave, to withdraw, to retire).

Chapter XVII

How after I Saw the Khan Off, I Returned to Ējmiatsin. On the Siege of the Fortress of Kars. How the Persians Cut Off the River and Deprived the Fortress of Water. How the Turks Promised to Surrender Erevan to the Persians. On the Khan's Visit to Tiflis and His Invitation for Us to Join Him There

Very early [in the morning] we departed from the camp and reached Ējmiatsin on Saturday, the eve of the feast of the Mother of God.[1] We arrived at the Holy See at night. In the morning, after services, we sat at the table and partook of the food supplied by the Khan and drank a cup in his honor.

After that [we began] to hurry our builders, whom the Khan had ordered to erect a dome on the hilltop where his tent had stood. He had commissioned Melik Mkrtum and me as managers of the project with all expenses having our approval. I could, however, appoint some responsible person to watch over the builders and the construction. [The Khan commanded the appointment] of two *mohtemeds*,[2] whom they call *sarkear*,[3] in order for them to record the expenses and to help the managers by ordering the transport of stones through the paths of surrounding villages. I appointed Ghalayji-Oğlı Step'anos Vardapet of Erzerum. He and Melik Mkrtum labored twenty days[4] on the hill until the construction was completed.

The construction was [finally] completed. It had the shape of a tent with a cupola on top. There was a cavity in [the copula], which, during rainfall allowed water to flow down the hill through a special chute. The construction was built in such a way that when the cavity became full, the water would flow down the chute into the gorge.

---

[1]August 16--for the Feast of the Assumption was on 17 August.

[2]Either *mo'tamen* (supervisor of expenses), or *mo'tamed* (trusted).

[3]*Sarkār* (overseer).

[4]Brosset (II, 276) has 40 days.

There was a village at the bottom of the gorge, which reportedly had been in ruins for more than a hundred years. The Khan sought the inhabitants of this village and gave them a writ[1]which made them tax-exempt,[2]permitting then to plough and sow 800 *somar* and not pay any *bahra* tax—that is *oshur*.[3]The village was rehabilitated and there are peasants living there today.

The Khan now advanced toward Kars and in a month's time had laid siege to it completely. He blocked the river, which irrigated and gave water to the city, and thus stopped the flow of water, which entered the fortress from the north through a conduit. He surrounded the city and laid siege to it from all sides.

In addition, prior to moving toward Kars, he dispatched [his cavalry] to carry out raids on two fronts, left and right. On one side, once more toward Bayazid, on the other side to Kaghzovan (Kagizman). He himself advanced in the middle. The above detachments ravaged the countryside, burned the buildings, took prisoners and livestock and, with a large booty returned to the main army in Kars. The Khan then dispatched his horsemen again and they reached the border[4]of Theodopolis.[5]They seized the regions of Nariman, Javakhēt',[6]Ch'ldir,[7]and Ghayi Ghulu,[8][all of which] were entirely populated by our people [Armenians]. They took away men, women, old people, and children, and, as was reported to us, drove some 6000 persons[9]to Ḵorāsān.[10]

The enemy then overcame its pride and conceit and a number of nobles left Erzerum and, in the capacity of envoys, went to see the

---

[1]The text has *raqam* (royal order).

[2]The text has *maf*, a corruption of *mu'af* or *mafaqa* (tax-exempt)

[3]*Bahra* implies *bahreh*, which was the share of the landlord or state under a crop-sharing agreement; *oshur* is the *'uşr* or one-tenth (of the produce paid for taxes).

[4]The text has *marz*.

[5]Refers to Thedosiopolis (Karin, Erzerum).

[6]In Akhalk'alak'i region, Georgia.

[7]A district in Kars, Turkey.

[8]A village in the Akhuryan region of Armenia.

[9]MSS. *c, e, f, v1* have the unlikely number of 1,000,000.

[10]The province in northeastern Iran.

Khan, who was still in the vicinity of Kars. After consulting with the grandees of Kars, they went to the Khan and begged and implored him not to totally destroy the land. They promised to surrender Erevan. The Khan was very glad, granted them *k̲al'ats*, and sent them together with a khan who was called …[1] in charge of a small number of horsemen to Erevan. Arriving in Erevan, he went to Bābā Khan, who was in K'alarē and who had the Khan of Erevan and Sardār Khan with him.

Taking some more men from [Bābā Khan] and another decree they entered Erevan, to persuade the Turks to peacefully surrender the fortress to the Khan.

After three or four days it became evident that [the Ottomans] would surrender the fortress, on the condition that the military supplies, that is the firearms in the arsenal, would be divided evenly: they [the Ottomans] would remove half and take it and half would remain in the fortress. An agreement was thus reached and it was affirmed [by an oath]. [The Ottomans] asked for carts to remove their belongings. They were granted 100 bullock-carts from the countryside.[2] They loaded their goods and left the fortress on Monday, 22 September [1735], on the Fast of the Holy Cross of Varag.[3] The drivers [of the carts] took them up to the bank of the Akhurean River, that is, the Arpa Çay; the Turks had to make their own way from there to Kars, while the drivers and their carts returned to their own homes.

The Khan returned from Kars and turned toward Tiflis. Prior to his journey he sent a written order to the khan of Erevan stating, "Bring the caliph, *kalāntar*, meliks, the Erevan grandees and *kadk̲odās* and come with them to the bank of the Akhurean River." Since we were late in our departure and he [the Khan] was in a hurry to get to Tiflis, we did not manage to catch up to him on the way. Instead we followed his route and arrived in Tiflis a day after

---

[1]In MS *d* the khan is identifies as 'Abdul-bālī; in MSS. *c, e, f, g* as; MSS. *b and v2* added in margins as 'Abdul-bāšı.

[2]MS *g* has 600 carts.

[3]The Feast of the Holy Cross of Varag is celebrated on the third Sunday after the Feast of the Exaltation of the Holy Cross. The Fast commences the day after.

his [arrival]. We left Ējmiatsin and the city of Erevan on 1 October and arrived in the city of Tiflis[1] on 27[2] October [1735].

Chapter XVIII

On Our Audience with the Khan in Tiflis. How He Gave us Comfort and Entrusted Holy Ējmiatsin and I to the Khan of Erevan and Granted Us All the Necessary Decrees

When we appeared before the Khan he was very happy. He uttered many comforting words and gave useful orders with specific instructions. He publicly established the order. With lengthy and strict instructions, he particularly entrusted the Holy See and me to the Khan of Erevan and the grandees of the land, stating, " Make sure you do not insult or distress the caliph, for he prays [for us] and is our *tevachi.*[3] Do not oppress the Üç-Kilisa Monastery, do not demand the slaughter of sheep, lambs, or chickens at appropriate or inappropriate times; but be content with what is already prepared and offered to you."

He was satisfied with our people and thanked [the Armenians]. "They have served me sincerely, with all their ability and [each] in every way has served me faithfully. Do not dare to oppress the Armenian people or to harm them, for I shall punish those who do severely. If you do not wish [my wrath], all taxes, save for the *ǰizya*,[4] should be evenly divided among the Armenians and the Muslims."[5]

He made many other important and useful statements and after these he added, "Go now and [if] you have any requests write petitions and submit them to me, for such is my order." We sat down

---

[1] MSS. c, e, f, g, v1 have P'aytakaran instead of Tiflis.

[2] MS *d* has 7 October.

[3] *Tevāǰī* or *towǰī* was a prefect who was the keeper of accounts and who collected levies from the villagers.

[4] Poll tax paid by non-Muslims.

[5] The term used is *Kızılbaş* (*qezelbāš*), which in this case implies the Persians or the Muslims and not the followers of the Ṣafavids who wore red headgear.

and conferred and requested *raqams*, which we felt, were useful and needed. He granted us more than fifteen *raqams* and sent us back to Erevan in the Ararat Province, content.

Chapter XIX
On How Our Khan of Erevan Departed But I Stayed on in Tiflis. How I Tried to Save the Tiflis and Ararat Armenians from Exile and How with God's Help I Managed to Save the Armenians of Tiflis

After their departure I remained in Tiflis for three days, for the most powerful Khan had ordered that 300 families from Tiflis and an equal number from the Ararat Province be forcibly driven to Ḵorāsān. He ordered the Khan of Erevan, the kalāntar, and the melik to, upon their arrival [in Erevan], make a list of 300 families and forcibly and against their will remove them from their homes and drive them to Ḵorāsān. The same order was given [for the Armenians] in Tiflis. They began to make a list of the 300 families and gather them in a church. Many who had heard that they were on the list came to the church where I was staying, sobbing, mourning, and wailing to heaven. They cried, screamed, fell on the floor, and begged me to ask the Khan to free them from being driven to a foreign place.

I suffered and choked, seeing the sorrow of my people—men and women—my heart burned. Covered with bloodstained tears I bowed at the threshold of the grandees, prayed and begged them to spare the Armenians from this sorrow.

Thank God that the Khan's heart was softened for some reason and he let them [the Armenians] go. Instead he demanded that they pay 3,000 *tomans* and 3,000 *somars* of grain. They gave [the money and the grain] and were freed [from exile].

I also tried with all my effort to save the 300 Armenian families from the Ararat Province. But it was not possible. The Khan ordered that each family be given two bullocks from the treasury so that they could load and take whatever [of their belongings] they wished with them. Those who remained gave each family three bulls,[1] three cows,[2] copperware measuring three liters, three mattresses,[3] three blankets,[4] flour and grain, and one *toman* in cash, and thus they departed.

Chapter XX

How I Asked That a Mint[5] Be Established [in Erevan] to Mint Copper Coins, if Silver Coins Were Not Possible, and if [Silver Was] Found, then Silver Coins as Well. On the Seven Mulk[6] Villages from Which the Melik and Kalāntar Could Not Collect Taxes Without My Knowledge. On How I Visited the Monasteries of Sanahin,[7] Haghpat,[8] and Haghartsin[9]

After that I began to reflect on the welfare and problems of the land, for there were not enough coins and these were soon reduced further, became very scarce, and eventually disappeared altogether. Therefore, I asked the great and powerful Khan to order that a mint be established in Erevan. I petitioned this through Melik Hakobjan and the Khan immediately granted my request. He was very

---

[1]MS *f* has donkeys instead of bulls.

[2]MS *g* has 4 cows; MSS. *b* and *d* do not mention the cows.

[3]The text has *karped*, which is most probably floor mats, stuffed mattresses or cushions (*došak* in Persian).

[4]The text has *lehap*, which is a corruption of *leḥāf.*

[5]The text has *ẓarrāb-ḵāne*.

[6]*Mulk* (*molk, melk, arbābī*) signifies private holdings.

[7]The Sanahin Monastery complex is located on the right bank of the Debed River in the Tumanyan region of present-day Armenia (northern part of the country, bordering Georgia). It was built in the 10th century during the Bagratid period (buildings were added up to the 13th century). One of the most important architectural sites in Armenia, it was a center of learning during the Middle Ages.

[8]The main church of this monastery was built in 967, the rest of it was completed during the 12-13th centuries. It is located in the Tumanyan region. A library was built there in 1258.

[9]Located among the woods north of Dilijan, the monastery was established in the 10th century, with buildings added in the 12-13 centuries.

pleased by this and in the presence of the grandees he praised [me] and said, "Observe the caliph. He is an old and holy man, a very good person. Observe how he watches over the *ra'yat*[1] and how he brings benefit to the chancery. Let them [the secretaries] write a proper *raqam* and give it [to him]."[2] His command was right then and there obeyed and they handed me the decree.

I also asked that the *kalāntar* and the melik did not, without my consent or knowledge, permit any tax collector from the treasury to assess the lands.

First, the following seven settlements were made *mulks* of the Holy See: Ējmiatsin, Mastara, Frankanots', Oshakan, K'irashlu,[3] Dibak'lu, Chelebi (Çelebi), and Ghshlagh (Qešlāq, Kişlak). These *mulks* were renewed, and I received another *raqam* from the mighty Khan, which once more affirmed these *mulks* as belonging to the Holy See, according to previous decrees.[4]

---

[1]The term has many meanings: subjects, non-Muslim subjects of a ruler, peasants, anyone (or a group) who requires to be taken care of. Both the singular and the plural form (*ra'āyā*) are used interchangeably.

[2]The original text is in Turkish written in Armenian characters: *Indi bu khalifani gorupsz. Bir yakhshi pir k'ishi dur. Mubarak' k'ishi dur. Chokh yakhshi dur. Bakh k'i ham ṛahat'i ghayirur ham divan salinay vayday olur. Dē t'ēz rakhami yakhshi yazsnlar u vērsinlēr.* In a modern rendition it may sound like:: *Indi bu halifani görüpsız* (MS b and v2 have *görüpaş*). *Bir yahşi pir kişi dur. Mubarek kişi dur. Çok yahşi dur. Bah ki ham ra`iyyati* (could be *rahati*) *ğayurur ham divan saliha fayda odur. De tez indi (imdi) rakami yahşi yazsenlar (yazısınlar) ve versınler.*

[3]MSS. *b and d* have Kirazlu; MS *v2* has Kirachlu.

[4]Although the leaders of the Armenian Church had received various land grants in form of religious endowments (*waqf*) or private property (*mulk*) of the Church, as well as tax-exemptions (*mu'āf*), as early as 1305 (during the Ilkhanid period), the unstable conditions in the region (the campaigns of Timur, Aq Qoyunlu, Qara Qoyunlu, Ṣafavids, and the Ottomans) required the renewal of all such documents by the new dynasty or ruler. Usurpation by local officials was common. The problems continued to haunt the Church during the Afšār, Zand, and Qājār periods as well. It is not surprising, therefore, that the Church archives (incorporated into the Matenadaran Archives in Erevan) contain numerous documents which repeatedly grant land or tax-exemptions to various kat'oghikoi (in most cases the names of the same villages appear in decrees granted over two centuries), see H. D. P'ap'azyan, *Matenadarani Parskeren Vaveragrerê* (two

In addition I asked him [the Khan] to give me another *raqam* which stated that no one would harass the Armenian peasants—for they were Christians—and that the *kadḵodās* of these villages, would not collect dues from the poor peasants without my knowledge; for the *kadḵodās* had a bad habit of transferring their own burdens onto the shoulders of destitute peasants. The Khan immediately granted me the said decree as well as all the other decrees, which I requested. Up to now I have received more than thirty-five *raqams*.

After that I left Tiflis and traveled to the famed monasteries of Sanahin and Haghpat. Then I visited the monastery of Haghartsin and [soon after] I returned to Holy Ējmiatsin.

By the command of the great Khan, the khan of Erevan and I wrote to Kars, Erzerum, and other places. I wrote to my people [the Armenians], and we both wrote separately to the pasha of Kars, stating that "According to the command of the Great Khan he wishes that your august state proclaim throughout the land that a peace treaty has been concluded and that all merchants[1] can once again travel freely. Let them buy and sell without fear or uncertainty. Let everyone do as they please." I dispatched *kondaks*[2] [stating the above] to Kars, Erzerum, T'ōkhat', Bayazid, Van, and Baghēsh.

---

volumes of *farmāns* [royal decrees] and one volume of *qabālejāt* [land deeds], Erevan, 1956-1968. For the Qājār period, see Bournoutian, Khanate, *op. cit.* pp. 65-92. A number of volumes containing Persian documents from the Timurid, Aq Qoyunlu, Qara Qoyunlu, Ṣafavid, and Qājār periods have been published in Tehran (ten volumes have appeared from 1962 to 1992). Although they have little to do with the Armenians, these volumes, edited primarily by 'A. Nava'ī and R. Naṣīrī, are valuable records on the system of land tenure and taxes prevalent in Iran and Transcaucasia from the early fifteenth to the mid-nineteenth century.

[1]The text has *sowdāgar*, who were wholesale merchants.

[2]Official writs, bulls, briefs, or instructions of a kat'oghikos.

Chapter XXI

On My Arrival at Ējmiatsin. My Journey to Erevan to Congratulate the Khan of Erevan. How Ṭahmāsp Qolī Invited Us to the Moğān Steppe[1]

After that, while I was in Erevan to congratulate the khan of Erevan[2] on the occasion of his appointment and of officially assuming his position, an order, once again, arrived from the Great Khan. It commanded that the khan of Erevan leave Erevan and the Ararat province on the third day after the new moon[3] and travel to the Moğān Steppe, which was located fifteen travel days from Erevan. In his order [the Khan] also stated, "Bring the caliph, the notables, the *kalāntar*, the meliks, and a number of *kadḵodās*. Come to the Moğān Steppe[4] right away, for I plan to make a proper statement and wish to consult[5] with all of you."

I, therefore, began to prepare for the journey, which was to commence in four to five days. May Lord Jesus and the Almighty God assure from heaven our success and our peaceful return to the Holy See and to our homes. We shall rely on God and on your prayers. May they bring good will to the Great Khan's plan.

We are totally amazed and do not know why are we called to go there, only God knows the reason. Some say that he [the Khan] is planning to install the shah on the throne, others claim that he will ascend [the throne himself]. The real reason is unknown. But we

---

[1]The Moğān Steppe is located south of the Arax River, as well as south of the confluence of the Arax and Kura Rivers, in the present-day Azerbaijan Republic.

[2]Moḥammad Qolī Khan Mūsābeg replaced Ḥasan 'Alī Khan Qājār at the end of 1735.

[3]According to Brosset (II, 280) they were to leave on 7 December. This seems accurate for Abraham left four to five days earlier, on 3 December (see chapter XXII).

[4]The text has *çöl*, which translates as desert, arid, barren, wasteland, or wilderness. The Moğān, however, has some good pastures, hence steppe is more appropriate.

[5]He planned to convene a general assembly or national council (*qurulta'i*).

shall pray to God that [the Khan] does well and succeed in that which is to his advantage. Amen![1]

Chapter XXII[2]

On HowThe Khan of Erevan and I Journeyed to the Moğān

When the time for our departure to Moğān arrived, I once more traveled to Erevan to take care of some necessary business. I met with the khan, who was called Mehmetkuli (Moḥammad Qolī), He was born in the Goght' district[3]and belonged to the Musabegean clan.[4]His grandfather became an apostate during the time of Shah 'Abbās the Great[5]and this Moḥammad Qolī Khan, his grandson, managed to obtain the title of khan. I heard that only two or three khans remained from those who were appointed by Shah Ṭahmāsp,[6]the rest of the mighty khans he [Ṭahmāsp Qolī (Nāder)] had exterminated. The khan of whom I speak [Erevan] was one of those who survived. He, therefore, honored me to have lunch with him.[7]

---

[1]The last paragraph is written in the present tense.

[2]Beginning with this chapter, MS *a* changes its format. The first twenty-one chapters were designated as first, second, third...to the twenty-first. Chapter twenty-two and the remaining chapters (except for chapters 49 and 50) are identified as twenty-two, twenty- three, etc.

[3]In the historic Armenian province of Siwnik', presently divided between Armenia and Azerbaijan (Meghri region and Ordubad region respectively). Moses of Khoren calls it the land of singers.

[4]Armenian meliks of Siwnik'.

[5]Ṣafavid shah (1587-1629) responsible for modernizing Persia and once again extending its power into Transcaucasia. Although he forcibly took some 250,000 Armenians south of the Arax River (Armenians thus became a minority in parts of eastern Armenia), he and his immediate successors were partially responsible for the first sparks of the Armenian national revival in the 17th century.

[6]Shah Ṭahmāsp II (1722-1732) was the last Ṣafavid monarch. He was deposed by Nāder in 1732 and was killed (together with his sons) by Nāder's son Rezā Qoli in 1740 in Ḵorāsān.

[7]He was soon replaced by Pīr Moḥammad Khan.

After we had eaten and were full, while he was smoking his water-pipe[1] and I drank my tea, I said, "My khan, when do we leave for the Moğān Steppe. I need to make preparations."[2] He answered, "Caliph, we can leave in a several days' time."[3] I replied, "If that is so, I shall depart a few days earlier. I shall travel slowly for I am weak and shall not survive [the journey]. I shall spent a few days in Astabad[4] and Akulis[5] until you arrive and we shall then together travel to the Moğān."

He agreed to this and said, "Good, do so, but take a lot of provisions for people and animals, for you shall find none there.

I, therefore, rushed back to the monastery and busied myself with the preparations for the journey. I took ten camels, ten mules, and sixteen horses. I took [with me] from the congregation, Vardapet Step'annos Ghalaychizada,[6] the co-adjutant;[7] Vardapet Barsegh, the crozier;[8] Vardapet Eghiay of Kurdistan, from the monastery of Hndzuts', the horsemaster;[9] Vardapet Mkrtich' from Tat'ew, the official host;[10] Vardapet Khach'atur of Isfahan, the supervisor of reserve horses;[11] Vardapet Sargis, the keeper of stores (provi-

---

[1]The text has ghalion (*qalyān*).

[2]The text is in Turkish written in Armenian characters: *Khanum shindi nēch'agh gēt'magh olur Mughan ch'olinay k'i t'adarik gorlaum.* That is, *Khanım şindi (şimdi) neçağ gitmağ olur Moğān çölina ki tadarık göralüm.*

[3]The text is in Turkish written in Armenian characters: *Khalifay birghach' gundan soray get'mak olur.* That is, *Khalifa birğaç gündan sora (sonra) gitmağ olur.*

[4]Located by the bank of the Arax (in present-day Nakhichevan), it was, until the beginning of the twentieth century, a large Armenian village. A number of Armenian monuments (including remnants of churches) are still there.

[5]The center of Goght' district, presently in Nakichevan. Its Armenian inhabitants, like those in Julfa, were engaged in trade, mainly silk with Europe and Russia.

[6]In Chapters XVII and XL he is mentioned as Step'anos Ghalayji-oğlı.

[7]*The text has at'oṛakal.*

[8]The text has *gavazanakir*.

[9]The text has *imlakhor*, which is a corruption of *amīrāḵor*.

[10]The text has the Persian term *mehmāndār*, a person who was in charge of receiving and entertaining guests.

[11]The text has the Turkish term *yedekçi.*

sions);[1] the prior of the monastery of the Illuminator, Vardapet Sargis of Kayseri; two deacons: Ghukas and Khach'atur; the scribe Hovhannēs of Gamri,[2] three footmen (*šāṭers*): Mkrtum, Pōghos, and Maghakia; three camel drivers;[3] three grooms for the horses, and three mule drivers. In addition, I took from Akulis, the senior priest Father T'uman,[4] the village elder, a head cook[5]—altogether twenty-five persons.[6]

We departed from Ējmiatsin on 3 December and traveling through Noragavit,[7] Khor Virap, Sharur,[8] we reached Astabad in five days. [I arrived in Astabad] on Monday, 8 December, on the Fast of St. Hakob [of Nisibis]. I spent two nights there. After that I went up to the monastery and spent two additional nights. From there I traveled to the Monastery of St. Karapet in Erinjak[9] and spent a night there. I spent another night in Ts'ghnay.[10] On 11 December we reached Akulis and stayed there three days. Moḥammad Qolī Khan arrived. On 14 December [we] departed from Akulis and on the same day crossed the Arax and through Karadagh (Qarādāğ)[11] traveled to the Moğān. We arrived in Moğān, near the place where the Arax and Kura Rivers meet,[12] on Saturday

[1] The text has the Persian term the *'ambārdār.*

[2] MSS. *c, e, f, g, and v1* have Garis.

[3] The text has the Persian term *sarvān* (*sarban* in Turkish).

[4] Should be T'ovmay.

[5] The text has *aşçı başı.*

[6] MS *v1* has 27 persons.

[7] A village on the road between Erevan and Artashat, presently within the boundaries of greater Erevan.

[8] A district within the Ayrarat region of historic Armenia. It was part of the Sharur district during the khanate and is presently in Nakhichevan.

[9] A monastery is located in the historic province of Siwnik' and is currently in Nakhichevan.

[10] A village near Akulis.

[11] The highlands which separate Iranian Azerbaijan from the Arax River and eastern Armenia.

[12] The location of the camp was near J̌avād (present-day Sabirabad, Azerbaijan) which bordered on the north by the Kura and on the east by the Arax rivers, immediately to the west of the point of their confluence.

of Advent.[1] We left Ējmiatsin on 3 December and arrived in the Persian camp in the Moğān on 3 January [1736].

Chapter XXIII

On the Celebration of Christmas in Moğān and the Liturgy of the Blessing of the Water at the Bank of the Arax during the Commencement of the Year 1185[1736][2]

The deputy of the Great Khan, who supervised and kept watch over all the affairs of the troops in the camp, that is the *nasaqçı-başı* ʻAbd ol-Ḥasan Beg,[3] lodged us somewhat to the side of the camp, in cabins made of reeds. Over 500 cabins were prepared on the northern side of the camp for the various khans who were present on the bank of the Arax.[4] The day of the Eve of Epiphany [Armenian Christmas Eve] we went on an outing on horseback and saw the place where the Arax and the Kura meet. There were two[5] bridges there: One over the Arax before the location of the confluence, and the other, over the Kura, after the confluence of the two rivers. There was a fortification built over small boats,

[1]The Feast of the Nativity (Epiphany) was on Tuesday, 6 January 1736. The Saturday preceding it was 3 January.

[2]It is important to note that although the Armenian year had begun in September, Abraham uses the universal month of January as the start of the New Year in this chapter. It is possible that he realized the significance of the occasion and wished to date it accordingly.

[3]He was, as noted, the commander of Nāder's bodyguard. His troops now acted as the military police in the camp.

[4]Abraham must have counted only his section of the camp, for Mīrzā Mahdī states that there were some 12,000 buildings of wood and reeds, together with rest houses, mosques, meydāns, bazaars and baths. In addition, superb apartments for himself, his harem, his retinue, and craftsmen (*buyutāt*) were also built, *op. cit.*, p. 267. The large number of buildings are understandable considering that there were some 100,000, delegates, troops, and servants, *Ibid.* Father Bazin has 15,000 delegates, while Moḥammad Moḥsen has 20,000 delegates (quoted in Lockhart, *op. cit.*, p. 97).

[5]MSS. *b* and *d* do not have two.

which consisted of wooden launches[1] that were placed on the water beside each other over the span of the river. Thick ropes tied the launches to each other from one end to the other. The ends of the ropes were attached on the top to chains and on the bottom with ropes which resembled the thick cables of the mooring of galleons. Thick logs and boards, attached by nails covered the launches so that people could cross [the river].[2]

On both sides of the bridge across the Kura River, however, edifices and towers were constructed which resembled forts. They had installed artillery in these forts so that the enemy could not attack unexpectedly and damage the bridge. In addition guards were stationed to protect the bridge day and night. No one could cross the bridge without permission, for that was the road to Shemakhi (Šemāḵī),[3] Lezgistan (Daghestan),[4] Derbent (Darband),[5] that is Demir-Kapu (Iron Gates), Azhdarkhan (Astrakhan),[6] Moscow, and to the land of the Huns, that is the Tatars.

The bridge over the Arax, however, was on the road to Karabagh,[7] Tuzagh(Dizak),[8] Gēnchebasan and Gēnchu,[9] which extended

---

[1]The text has *ch'ẹrnêkh*, which is from the Bulgarian *chyrnykh* (wooden launch).

[2]The description resembles the fortified and sometimes covered bridges of the late Middle Ages.

[3]Also appears as Shemakha or Shemakh, the city was the center of Shirvan. It was a major trading center during the rule of the Shirvanshahs and continued as such until the appearance of Nāder. Since the Khan of Shemakhi had allied himself with the Lesghians and the Ottomans and would not submit to Persia, Nāder destroyed the town and moved most of its inhabitants to a new location nearby. The new town is referred to as New Shemakhi in some sources.

[4]The Lesghians and other mountain tribes lived in Daghestan, which is a region in the eastern Caucasus. The various tribes of that region had a tradition of autonomy and have resisted many conquerors.

[5]The port of Derbent is the gate to the Caspian littoral.

[6]Astrakhan is a port at the mouth of the Volga, where it connects to the Caspian Sea.

[7]Karabagh is the Turkish name for the historic Armenian province of Artsakh. MSS. *c, e, f, v1* have Karadagh (Qarādāğ) instead of Karabagh.

[8]Dizak is one of the five districts of Mountainous Karabagh, which was populated predominantly by Armenians.

[9]Most likely, the khanate and the city of Ganǰe.

to Gandzasar,[1] Kap‘an (Qapan),[2] and Sisian (Siwnik‘). Therefore, they [the Persians] did not concern themselves with its protection. They stationed only a few men to assure that the prisoners of war would not escape.

After visiting all of this, we returned to our quarters, which were an hour's distance from the confluence of the Arax and Kura Rivers, for the bridge across the Arax was [located] within the area where the army was stationed, while the bridge across the Kura was below the camp and we were stationed in the upper part of the camp.

Next day, on a Tuesday,[3] we pitched a large tent, which we had brought from Holy Ējmiatsin and which resembled a church, having a cupola-like top and decorated with drawings, crosses and flowers. I ordered that all born [to the faith of] the Illuminator [Armenians] to gather there and those [Armenian soldiers] who were in the camp to come to my tent the next day [Christmas Day]. On Christmas Day they all came to my tent and we celebrated the feast of the birthday of Christ, Our Lord. We did so without an altar or liturgy, without any spiritual satisfaction, with heavy sorrow and tears, just like the ancient Israelites who hung their harps on willows.[4] Thus with sad faces and broken hearts our people against my will dressed me and taking the few church vessels and religious utensils we had brought we us, which were indispensable for a religious procession, I, together with priests, deacons, and lectors,[5] dressed in robes and carrying lit candles descended from the tent to the Arax.

There we performed the ceremony of the preparation of holy water by pouring the holy *meṛon* in the waters of the Arax. The

---

[1] Gandzasar was the center of the kat‘oghikosate of Aghuank‘.

[2] Kap‘an is a town in the region of Zangezur (present-day Armenia).

[3] Brosset interprets this as Tuesday eve.

[4] Refers to *Psalms* 137: 2 "On the willows there we hung up our harps." Although Psalm no. 137 is a lament and a prayer for vengeance on Israel's enemies, it also states that it is difficult to sing the Lord's praise when living among foreigners or unbelievers."

[5] The text has *dprok‘*, which also translates as "reader" or "seminarian."

kalantar of Erevan, Melikjan, Melik Hakobjan, Melik Mkrtum, Melik Ēgēn (Egan] of Dizak were present. At my command he [Melik Egan] removed the cross from the water.[1] In addition [there were] the *kadḵodās* of Erevan and the Ararat province, the Armenian [soldiers or officials] in the army, the *āqā* of Erevan, and distinguished people, such as the *sheikh ul-Islam*,[2] the *qāẓī*,[3] and the Khan's *yüz-başı*;[4] altogether more than 300 Armenians and Muslims. The amazing thing was that the Persians took the water mixed with the *meṛon* and anointed their faces with it. I then left them and they went to their own places. We returned to our tent. There were some distinguished people with us whom we had invited to dine with us.

Chapter XXIV
On My Journey to Dizak and On My Immediate Return. On the Arrival of the Valīne'mat [5]

Snow fell on Christmas Day and continued to fall during that night [and] made us suffer. Therefore, on the second day after the sanctification of the water, I hurried to cross the bridge and travel to Dizak. I first went to the khan of Erevan, who lived in one of the reed huts, in the same part of the camp as we. I told him, "Since the mighty Khan is not here and it is not known when will he arrive, I wish to go to Dizak, for we and our animals are dying from the cold. The moment I am informed of the arrival of the Khan I shall

---

[1] The ceremony reenacts the Baptism of Jesus by dipping the cross in the hallowed water.

[2] Chief religious authority of a region.

[3] From the Arabic *qadhi*, judge of a *Šari'a* court.

[4] A captain, commander in charge of 100 men.

[5] From here on Abraham abandons the use of the *Khan* or Ṭahmāsp Qolī, and uses one of the titles of Nāder, that of *Valīne'mat*, which translates as "Lord of Beneficence." By this time, however, the Persians and the Ottomans viewed him as the Regent or Lord Protector.

hasten my return." The khan did not wish to let me go, for he did not wish to remain alone.

I did not heed his wish and rushed to the commander of the camp, 'Abd ol-Ḥasan Beg, informing him of my wish. He immediately got on his horse and came to our quarters to ascertain if there were enough huts for our needs or more had to be constructed. For that reason he met with the khan of Erevan and during their conversation he commented, "I do not know [when] the Great Khan will arrive. There are many provisions missing from this place and you are ill. What do you wish to do?" The khan responded. "What can I do? I am afraid to go somewhere, in case [the Khan] returns and, not finding me here, orders my execution. The caliph [also] wishes to leave, but I did not permit him to do so." 'Abd ol-Ḥasan Beg answered, "Do not detain the caliph. He is old and ill. Let him travel to Dizak. When our leader arrives he shall return, for [the Khan] loves him and therefore will not harm him in any way."

He then got on his horse and on the way to his quarters met me on the road and said, "Caliph! For your sake I rode to your khan [of Erevan] and spoke to him about you. You can go wherever you wish, but the instant you hear of the arrival of the Great Khan, hasten to return. I shall construct another reed cabin, a large one, so that on your return you shall be housed comfortably. Blessing the mighty Khan and thanking the beg, I replied, "Very well, I shall go and shall return immediately when I learn of the arrival [of the Khan]. As far as the cabin is concerned, do not concern yourself with it, for the quarters built for us are sufficient for our needs and there is no need to built more."

Rain mixed with snow was falling when I left. Traveling in terrible mud I arrived by the bridge over the Arax and rushed to Dizak. But the *kalāntar* and melik [of Erevan] upon crossing the bridge remained there, for there were troops camped[1] on that side as well. They stopped at the [tent] of the book-keepers,[2] who were

[1] The text has *orduci*, who were not part of the regular fighting forces, but were craftsmen who accompanied the army. The Persians referred to them as the members of the *buyutāt*.

[2] The text has *mīrzās*.

the controllers[1] of Erevan sent by the treasury[2] and who had to examine certain accounts[3] with them.[4]

The next morning when the *kalāntar* and the melik set off to follow me, they heard that the mighty Khan would arrive in five or six days. They informed me of this by courier. Hearing this I turned back, for I had [at least] a two-day journey ahead of me.

I reached the [outskirts of] camp on the eighth day of Christmas on a Monday.[5] I found out that the second Alexander [Nāder] had arrived a day earlier on Sunday night.[6] Since it was evening when I crossed over the bridge on the Arax, where the *kalāntar* and the melik together with the accountants were waiting in their tent, I spent the night there.[7]

---

[1]The text has *ẓābeṭ* (revenue officer, controller).

[2]The text has *mīrī* (state treasury).

[3]The text has *hisab* (*ḥesāb*).

[4]Throughout the *Chronicle* Abraham makes numerous references to the strict accountability of various provincial officials regarding the taxes collected for the central *dīvān*. Since the withdrawal of the Ottomans had left western Transcaucasia in the hands of local khans, Nāder sought immediately to place them under his control. Thus, he managed to collect the much-needed revenues for his future campaigns, as well as the great expense he was to incur for the gathering of the national council.

[5]12 (23 N.S.) January 1736 according to Brosset (II, 284).

[6]Abraham's record of the date of Nāder's arrival is corroborated by Mīrzā Mahdī, *op. cit.*, p. 267. With a few exceptions, the dates of events recorded in the *Chronicle* are accurate and should be considered as a definitive source by scholars of the history of Iran in the eighteenth century.

[7]Lockhart in error assumes that Abraham arrived in the camp—for the first time—on the 23rd, a day after Nāder's arrival (22 January), *op. cit.*, p. 97. The text makes it clear that Abraham had arrived in the Moğān much earlier (14 January N.S.). After settling in his quarters, he had decided to visit some Armenian settlements in Karabagh, and had hurried back the moment he had heard of Nāder's arrival.

Chapter XXV

On Our Meeting with the Great Khan, the Presentation of Our Gifts, Our Conversation with Him and His Assurances to Us

Early Tuesday morning we readied ourselves and rushed across the bridge to the part of the camp where the great Khan's headquarters and court were located. I, together with the *mīrzās*, *kalāntar* and meliks, as well as the *āǧā* of Erevan, the *sheikh ul-Islam*, our *kadḵodās*, and other noted people were all gathered together and taken into the presence of the mighty Khan. They honored me by presenting me first. My gifts—horses, mules, and other items, which I had brought with me—were brought forth.

Seeing this, the Khan was moved, and glad to see me, he said, "Welcome caliph! How are you? Do you feel well? Are you sound and healthy? Did you meet with any injuries on your journey due to the winter and snow? You are [after all] an old man. Have you been here long?[1] I replied, "My Khan, may Allah grant you a long life. Now that I have seen your perpetually mighty and blessed face, the winter has turned into spring. Thank God that I see your majesty unharmed, healthy, and bright."[2]

---

[1]The original text is in Turkish with Armenian letters as follows: *Khosh galmish san khalifay. Nējay san. Yakhshi san. Ch'aghsan, Yolday azar chak'mishsan ghshdan ghardan, chun bir ēkhtiar kishi sēn. Ch'okhdan galmish-san*. The following is an approximate rendition of the above if written in the Ottoman script and transliterated into modern Turkish orthography: *Hoş gelmiş san halifa. Nece san? Yahçi san? Çağ san? Yolda azar çağmiş san kışdan kar-dan? Çun bir ehtiyar kişi sen. Çoktan gelmiştan.*"

[2]The original text is in Turkish written in Armenian letters: *Khanêm Alah sanay chokh omr vērsn. Indi ki sēnin mubarak' lēylinhar shēfkēt'li uzun gordum, ghêsh manay bhar oldi. Shukur p'ērvērdikaray, ki bēn jēnabni sagh, sēlim vē urushan geordum*. The following is also an approximate rendition of the above if written in the Ottoman script and transliterated into modern Turkish orthography: *Khanım Allah sana çok ömr (ömür) varsın. Indi ki senin mübarek leyli-nehar şevketli yüzün kardan ğeş mana bahar oldi. Şükur (şükr) perverdegara* (from the Persian *parvardehgār*) *ki ben cenabni (cenap) sağ, salim, ve u'ruşen. gördum.*"

He laughed happily and said, "'Abd ol-Ḥasan Beg find the caliph good lodgings. Take care of him, for he is a venerable old man."[1]

After that, gifts from the others, the *kalāntar*, the meliks, and the *āqā*, were presented [to the Khan]. The Khan thanked them and said, "Welcome and may your homes be prosperous."[2] He then turned to all of us and said, "Go and rest."[3] We all bowed our heads, saluted him, and returned to our former quarters.

On the same day, in the evening, he [the Khan] sent one of his servants and summoned me to his presence. I took the *kalāntar* and hurried to see the mighty Khan in his court. They informed him of my arrival and he called me in right away. I, together with the *kalāntar*, stood before him. He asked us about [conditions] in the various districts of the Erevan [province], about Kars, about the movement of [trade] caravans, about Bayazid, and the land of Kurdistan. I gave him appropriate answers and to show my gratitude and contentment I said, "Thanks to God and thanks to your rule and [administrative] care we have a peaceful existence in every possible way. In addition, by your decree granted to the khan [of Erevan] and me in Tiflis, we sent notices encouraging travelers to our region. Moreover, I wrote a petition[4] to the pasha of Kars and to the *sar'askar* of Erzerum, Ahmet Pasha, regarding merchants [trade]. Thus caravans have begun to arrive and merchants, both our nationals and Ottoman, have come [to trade]. In fact, very soon we expect the arrival a number of large caravans [to Erevan]."

He asked, "What about the khan of Erevan? Does he administer well? Does he treat you well? Does he show concern in his job? Are you satisfied with him?" I thanked him and replied, "He is good in every way. He conscientiously performs the affairs and duties of his office."

---

[1]The text is in Turkish written in Armenian letters: *Abdul-Hasan Bek, khalifiay yakhshi otakh vēr yakhshi gozat', bir yakhshi ghojay kishi dur.*"

[2]The text is in Turkish written in Armenian letters: *Ēvênz avadan. Khosh galmishsz.*

[3]The text is in Turkish written in Armenian letters: Varun *rahat' olun.*

[4]The text had *'arẓa.*

He then asked me about the regions of Bayazid, Kurdistan, and Kars and his heart was content with my answers. Finally he asked about the plowing and sowing. I complained immediately stating, "[Our plowing and sowing is] not sufficient. We also lack bulls for tilling. Let it be your wish that in spring the administration procure bulls from Bayazid or Kars, through purchase or borrowing, and thus we can till and sow the fields. The spring plowing is accompanied by [extensive] irrigation and should produce a good harvest."

He [the Khan] had already sent a certain man called Kalb 'Alī Beg, who [unbeknown to us] had gone throughout the Ararat province and had checked the plowing and sowing in all the villages. He had recorded the number of bulls and the amount of seed. He had visited Ējmiatsin as well and had ordered that the [inhabitants of] *mulk* villages be given seed from the monastery. He had impelled them [the monastery officials] to do so, threatening that otherwise the state would have to give them seeds and the [*mulk*] villages would then belong to the state. I do not know if he [the Khan] asked all this to test me, to find out if I was telling the truth, or if he was concerned about the land and the *ra'yats*. After that he reassured me stating, "Do not worry, I know that is so. God is kind and you shall not have any need. He then said, "You are free (*morraḵas*)! Go to your lodging and pray. We exited and in the dark returned to our cabins.

Chapter XXVI
On My Visiting the Tent of the Nakhichevanis, that is Paron Astuatsatur, Paron Kharisimos, and Paron Step'an and On How I Conferred with Them Regarding Certain Affairs

The next day, at noon, when I was on my way to the tent of the Nakhichevanis, where they had taken shelter in the camp, on the bank of the Arax River, I met servants of the almighty Khan, who were called *farrāš*.[1] These were two men, each of whom had a lamb in his arms. Seeing me they stopped and when I approached they moved towards me and stood in my way. I greeted them and asked, "What do you want?" They answered, "May you be healthy! The Alexander-like Khan has sent this lamb for you to taste and to bless the Khan. I asked, "And to whom are you taking the second lamb?" They answered, "This one is for the khan of Erevan." I thanked them and astride my horse I made the sign of the cross and blessed the Khan. I gave a gold piece to the one that had brought the lamb and rode further.

Two days later, on 16 January, the great Khan ordered that all present should receive a salary. Every three men got one Tabrīzī liter of grain, that is two *okka*[2] and 100 *dram*.[3]

On 18 January, on Sunday, Paron Astuatsatur from Astabad invited me to his tent to a celebration in my honor. While I was sitting at the table in the tent, I learned that they had just raised a large tent brought especially from Qazvīn.[4] I remained there until two o'clock in the morning and we then returned to our lodging.

Oh, the great and mighty rule of the second Alexander! For the entire large army, composed of many different people, like a single man, stood silently, modestly, and trembling. Not a single man dared to utter a word to his companion or [even] a camp follower. They did not even order our people [the Armenians], "Do this or that." Every man was concerned about his own safety and seized with fear.

On 20 January Ganǰ 'Ali Pasha,[5] the Turkish envoy, arrived from Ganǰe. He was housed on the other side of the Arax, on the

---

[1] Chamberlain or butler, literally "one who spreads carpets."

[2] *Okka* (*oqqe*) is a Turkish measure equal to 400 *dirhams* or 2.83 lbs.

[3] From the Greek *drachma* (*dirham*), a monetary and weight (one-eighth of an ounce or 60 grains, or one-sixteenth of avoirdupois weight) unit.

[4] It is a major city in northern Iran, on the road between Tehran and Tabrīz. It served as the capital of Iran during the 16th century.

[5] 'Alī Pasha was the former governor of Ganǰe, who had surrendered the citadel following the battle of Eghvard.

bank of the river, near the place where the Arax met the Kura River.

On 22 January Ebrahim Khan,[1] who was the brother of the mighty Khan, arrived from Mašhad.[2] He was as burly and as tall as his brother was.

The same day the khan called Alexander [Nāder] sent me *k̲al'ats* consisting of two magnificent omophorions,[3] each was worth fifty[4] *tomans*.[5] They were trimmed with fur all around. Among the many omophorions in Holy Ējmiatsin, there were none to match their quality. Each of them had twelve images that were woven at the same time as the cloth, not embroidered afterwards. Among them were six [different] images of Christ; a representation of the [tomb] and resurrection; according to the four[6] evangelists and the arrival of women bearing chrism [at the tomb].

Two [of the twelve] portrayed the appearance of the disciples [of Christ, at the tomb]. The first was based on Luke: "Peter got up and ran to the tomb; stooping and looking in, he saw the linen cloths by themselves; then he went home, amazed at what had happened."[7]

The second image was based on John: "Then Peter and the other disciple set out and went toward the tomb. The two were running together."[8]

The six other images were as follows:[9] In the circle with the image of Jesus Christ, the Lord is making the sign of the cross with

---

[1]Moḥammad Ebrāhīm Khan, known as Ẓahīr al-Dowleh was made the commander-in-chief of Azerbaijan after Nāder's coronation. He was killed by the Lesghians in 1738.

[2]The main city of the province of K̲orāsān in northeastern Iran.

[3]The text has *emip'oron*, a vestment resembling the pallium of the Latin Church, worn by patriarchs and bishops.

[4]MS *v1* has 10 *tomāns*.

[5]A *tomān* was worth 10,000 *dirhams*.

[6]MSS *c, e, f, v1* have no four.

[7]*Luke*: 24.12.

[8]*John*: 20.3-4. The entire text of *John* 20.4 reads, "but the other disciple outran Peter and reached the tomb first."

[9]Abraham counts this as the seventh image of the twelve.

both hands. Around the circle [with the image] of Jesus Christ, there were eight smaller circles. Four of them had the icons [symbols] of the four evangelists: a man, a lion, an ox, and an eagle. In a small circle above the head of Jesus Christ was the Holy Spirit. In the sixth circle, below Christ, there was a six-winged seraphim. The small circle on the right of [Christ] contained an image of the Holy Virgin Mary. The small circle on the left [of Christ] was the image of St. John the Baptist.

The eighth image located at the lower end of the omophorion, portrayed Christ with his hands on the heads of the apostles blessing them on Mount of Olives on the day of Ascension. The ninth image was based on the gospel of John:[1]"They gave Him a piece of broiled fish and a honeycomb. And when he had eaten in their presence, he took what remained and gave it to them."[2]

The tenth image described the passage in which Christ came through shut doors and spoke with Thomas ["Although the doors were shut, Jesus came and stood among them and said, "Peace be with you." Then he said to Thomas, "Put your finger here and see my hands. Reach out your hand and put it in my side. Do not doubt but believe." Thomas answered him, "My Lord and my God! Jesus said to him, "Have you believed because you have seen me? Blessed are those who have not seen and yet have come to believe."][3]

The eleventh image was based on [the gospel of] John in which Christ appeared by the Sea of Tiberias and spoke to Peter and Nathanael, sons of Zebedee and two other disciples and helped them to fish and have the fish and bread broiled on coal ["After those things Jesus showed himself again to the disciples by the Sea of Tiberias; and he showed himself in this way. Gathered there together were Simon Peter, Thomas called the Twin, Nathanael of Cana in Galilee, the sons of Zebedee, and two others of his disciples. Simon Peter said to them, "I am going fishing." They said to

---

[1]The text has John but the quotation is from Luke, a surprising error on the part of Abraham, as well as the copiers, who were priests.

[2]*Luke*: 24.42-43.

[3]*John*: 20.26-29.

him, "We will go with you." They went out and got into the boat, but that night they caught nothing. Just after daybreak, Jesus stood on the beach; but the disciples did not know it was Jesus. Jesus said to them, "Children, you have no fish, have you?" They answered him, "No." He said to them, "Cast the net to the right side of the boat, and you will find some." So they cast it, and now they were not able to haul it in because there were so many fish. That disciple whom Jesus loved said to Peter, "It is the Lord!" When Simon Peter heard that it was the Lord, he put on some clothes, for he was naked, and jumped into the sea. But the other disciples came in the boat, dragging the net full of fish, for they were not far from the land, only about a hundred yards off. When they had gone ashore, they saw a charcoal fire there, with fish on it and bread. Jesus said to them, "Bring some of the fish that you have just caught." So Simon Peter went aboard and hauled the net ashore, full of large fish, a hundred fifty-three of them; and though there were so many, the net was not torn. Jesus said to them, "Come and have breakfast." Now none of the disciples dared to ask him, "Who are you?" because they knew it was the Lord. Jesus came and took the bread and gave it to them, and did the same with the fish."[1]

The twelfth image, which was located at the other end of the omophorion, portrayed the investiture and transfer of the keys [of heaven] to Peter.

These were the images on the most valuable omophorion, which weighed 750[2] *dirhams*. The other omophorion was made of black damask silk[3] and had seven[4] crosses made of gold and pearls. These magnificent crosses were heavy and were embroidered on the omphorion. I present this burdensome enumeration to describe all the images and pictures.

I also [received] a fur-lined pouch, which closely resembled our

---

[1]*John*, 21.1-13.

[2]MS *a* does not have 750; *g* has 700; *v2* has 700 but 50 has been added later.

[3]The text has *kamḵā*.

[4]MS *d* has 5 crosses.

konk'er.[1] In the center of the pouch was an image of Christ, making the sign of the Cross. On the four corners were the images of the four evangelists.

In return I granted them [the two messengers] *k̲al'ats* and gifts according to my means. For the two were among his most intimate attendants and by his orders had carried the gifts [from the Khan] in their hands and had placed them in front of me. They had [respectfully] saluted me in the name of the great Khan and had devotedly asked the state of my health. Fearing the Khan, they at first refused to accept my gifts, but I eventually forced them to take them. I assured them and said, "I shall not utter a word to anyone regarding this matter and you should not tell your friends about this either." They then were convinced and with great hesitation they finally took them. For the Muslim Khan had made it known that if he sent something to someone and those who carried the item requested something in return or took something in exchange, they would be mercilessly put to death. They left and returned to the place of their servitude. The khan of Erevan and his entire camp, which were my neighbors, learned of and saw the gifts from the Khan and were full of rapture and astonished at the love the Khan had for me and of his generosity toward me. They visited me daily and congratulated me. The gifts were admired by all. Glory to God and Blessed Be His Name. For He alone creates miracles.

Chapter XXVII

On The Description of the Tent that was Brought from Qazvīn. How they Erected it So That We Could Appear for the Daily Salām before the Khan. On How They Prepared Sitting Places for Those Who Came for the Daily Salām.

After that the mighty Khan ordered that I, the khan of Erevan, and all our followers, present ourselves each sunrise for the daily

[1] A type of rectangular pouch suspended over the thigh, worn by the patriarch or his representative.

salām.[1] Close to the Khan's quarters and court, they prepared sitting places from reeds, resembling a *ṣundurma,*[2] which in these parts is called *'eyvān*, measuring ten, fifteen and twenty girths long and two girths wide. Men from each city, together with their fellow citizens, sat separately under these porticos. Early in the morning we went to [the place] erected for us. Each person knew his place, which was prepared for him [in advance].

In the third hour [after sunrise] the almighty Khan would come out from the interior to the *dīvānḵāne*[3] and [after] the *çavuş*'[4] performed the prayer,[5] all, in order, would pass him [the Khan], bend their head, would greet him silently, and would move along.

The Khan's court was constructed of wood and its roof was made of boards. The neighboring lodge, fences, and the quarters for the women and the interior were made of rush.

Inside the court of the Khan there were many tents. The same was true of our quarters, which were situated inside the camp at the turn of the bank of the Arax River. Half an hour's ride from the camp, were more than 500 cabins made of reed. Some of the khans had originally wished to camp there, but since these huts were far from the Khan's headquarters, they were not allowed to do so and were housed around the living quarters of the Khan.

After two or three days there came an order from the great Khan, that I and all those who had come from Erevan go to see the tent[6] and be entertained. After us almost all the others rushed to see the gigantic tent and to admire it. This very large tent, which was brought from Qazvīn was surrounded by a fence made of reeds and

---

[1] To sit and receive in state, traditional salutations of health and peace uttered by those visiting a ruler during the start of daily ceremonies, a feast day, or the beginning of the New Year.

[2] Turkish word for awning or open shed

[3] Persian word for audience hall.

[4] Turkish term meaning beadle, sergeant, herald, or halberdier of the royal guard.

[5] The text has *du'ā.*

[6] The text has *çadır* (*čādor*).

was pitched near the harem, west of the apartments[1] of the Khan. It was some 110[2] *ḥalebi*[3] long, 50[4] *ḥalebi* wide, and 18 *ḥalebi* high and adorned with cupolas. There were twenty pillars inside the tent, each crowned with silver knobs [crossbars], the size of medium watermelons. Each had a symbol that looked like ↓.[5] The tent was of a reddish purple color on the outside and had a double lining—the first solid and unbroken, the second carved cage framework.[6] Inside [of the tent] the covering was stitched with silk from Gīlān.[7] We beheld (*tamāšā*) the tent, admired it, and thanking God returned to our quarters.

Chapter XXVIII
On How Every Day Men of Different Ranks Would Come from Afar to the Moğān Steppe

Invited guests began to arrive from all directions. First [to arrive] was Pīr Moḥammad Khan of Herāt[8] whom the [mighty Khan] appointed, upon his arrival in the Moğān, as the [new] khan and *beglarbegi* of Erevan; but whom nonetheless he [the Khan] has kept by his side. In his place he has appointed another person, a *muteselim*,[9] or as they call him in these parts, *na'ib*,[10] Moḥammad

[1] The text has otağ [oṭāq], which in this case is not a room but a state tent.

[2] MS *v1* has 140.

[3] Cloth measure of 20 to 30 inches long.

[4] MS *v1* has 10; *a* is missing 50.

[5] The above symbol closely resembles the symbol in the text, which is slightly concave.

[6] The text has *mahacar kafes oyma.*

[7] The text has *Gilanu ghanavet ghumash*, which is *kanava* (canvas for embroidering), *gümüş* (silvery).

[8] Refers to Pīr Moḥammad Khan of Marv, the *beglarbegi* of Herāt, who replaced Moḥammad Qolī Khan.

[9] The title can best be translated as Lt. Governor; from the *Arabic mutesallim*, someone who is sent to manage the affairs of a place until the arrival of his superior.

[10] A deputy or a lieutenant.

Reżā Beg,[1] whom he dispatched from Moğān and who to this day is in Erevan administering the Erevan province for Pīr Moḥammad Khan.

[Thereafter arrived] the *Vakīl* of K̲orāsān, Tamaz[2] [Ṭahmāsp] Khan,[3] the *sardār*[4] of all of Iran, that is the *sar'askar*; the *mīrzās*[5] of Māzandarān: the *vakīl*,[6] *vazīr*,[7] and *mīrsofī*,[8] that is, the *baş* (head) *daftardar*,[9] the *baş muhasib*,[10] and the *baş mankvat*,[11] for every region in the country has these three officials.

The *mīrzās* of Nīšāpūr: *vakīl*, *vazīr*, *mīrsofī*.

Ebrāhīm Khan of Mašhad, the brother of the great Khan, the current *sepahsālār*, that is the *sar'askar* of all of Atrpatakan, or Azerbaijan.

The *mīrzās* of Sabzavār: *vakīl*, *vazīr*, *mīrsofī*.

Moḥammad Ḥosein Khan Qāǰār of Astarābād.[12]

The *mīrzās* of Gīlān: *vakīl*, *vazīr*, and *mīrsofī*.

Moḥammad Reżā Khan of Qazvīn.

Qāsem Khan of Qom.

The *mīrzās* of Kāšān.

---

[1] Moḥammad Reżā Beg K̲orāsāni (Pasākūhī). According to Moḥammad Kāżem, Nāder appointed him, a trusted *mīn-başı* (commander of a thousand) of his bodyguard, to this position, *op. cit.*, I, folio 310b.

[2] MSS. *a, c, e, f, v1,* and *v2* have Taham.

[3] Refers to Ṭahmāsp Khan J̌alāyer, the *Vakīl al-dowle*, a close confidant of Nāder. In this case *vakīl* translates as vice-regent.

[4] Commander of all the land forces, commanding general.

[5] The term has a number of meanings: when placed before a name it signifies a scribe, private secretary, or chief accountant of the treasury; when placed after a name it identifies the person as a royal prince.

[6] Arabic *wakil*, Turkish *vekil*, which translates as counselor, agent, or purveyor.

[7] Arabic *wazir*, Turkish *vezir* was an officer of the state, an assistant to the governor. Ministers were also called *vazīr* (vizier) and the main official of the land was the grand vizier or Prime Minister.

[8] The correct term is *mostowfi* who was the controller or head clerk.

[9] *Defterdar*, or keeper of financial records.

[10] Accountant, auditor.

[11] The correct term is *manqūlāt* (*mankulat*) or movable property.

[12] Probably Moḥammad Qolī Qāǰār, who was the *beglarbegī* of Astarābād.

Me'yār-başı Khan of Isfahan.[1]

Loṭf 'Alī Khan of Tehran.[2]

The grandees of Samrān,[3] where Shah Ṭahmāsp and his son Shah 'Abbās are imprisoned.

Aḥmad Khan of Šīrāz.[4]

'Alī Qolī Khan of Lār.

'Abdollāh Khan of Bandar.[5]

Āqā Bāqer, the *sursayatchi-başı*[6] of Kermān.

Bāqer Khan of Kāzrān of the Silsup'ur[7] tribe.

The *mīrzās* from Yazd: *vakīl*, *vazīr*, and *mīrsofī*.

'Alī Mardān Khan of Dovraz[8].

The Vali of Havuz,[9] who is a great khan.

'Abbās Qolī Khan of Šūštar

Esmā'īl Khan of Behbahān

Hajji Seif al-Dīn Khan Bayāt of Kermānšāh[10]

Moṣṭafā Khan of Hamadān

Bābā Khan of Ḵorramābād[11]

'Abd or-Razzāq Khan of Tabrīz[12]

---

[1] Abraham's spelling does not indicate if it was *me'yār*, *maiyār*, or *me'iar*, the first was in charge of the mint in the old capital, the second was the chief purveyor of that city, while the third was the chief assayer or money changer.

[2] The text does not indicate if he was the same person who was the commander of the advance troops. He could also be the chief of the Aḥmadlu-Afšār.

[3] According to Persian sources the last Ṣafavids were imprisoned in Sabzavār. There is a possibility that Abraham misspelled the town of Samnān.

[4] Possibly refers to Aḥmad Khan Baḵtīyārī.

[5] Refers to Bandar-e 'Abbās, the main port on the Persian Gulf.

[6] Refers to *siyursatčı başı*, the person in charge of gathering provisions (via taxes in kind) for the army.

[7] Abraham's spelling makes it difficult to identify this *oymāq*.

[8] Abraham's spelling makes it difficult to identify the place.

[9] Havuz is probably Havīzeh (in Māzandarān); it could also be Ḥouẓ, near Mašhad.

[10] Also known as Nīšāpūrī, Missing in MS *a*.

[11] Possibly Bābā Khan Čāpešlu.

[12] Possibly the former governor of Marāğe. Probably from the Dombolī tribe.

Moḥammad Qolī Khan of Sovuḵbūlağ[1]
Moḥammad 'Isā' Khan of Ūrumīye
Imam Qolī Khan of Ardebīl[2]
Reżā Khan of Nakhichevan[3]
Moḥammad Qolī Khan of Erevan
Ugurlu Khan of Ganǰe[4]
The Vālī of Tiflis, son of Imam Qolī Khan,[5] 'Alī Mīrzā[6] Khan
Sfahan (Sobḥān) Verdi Kīāḵūm Bek Khan of Kazakh
Heirat, the *beglarbegi* of Shemakhi[7]
Kalb Ḥosein Khan of Loṛi
Mortażā[8] Qolī Khan of Čors
The Sultan of Mākū
The *mīrzās* of Kakhet'i
Mūsā Khan Ṭālеši of Darband, that is Demir Kapu (Iron Gates)

They came from other distant places—from Ḵorāsān, from Bākū, from the southern regions, from the land of the K'anans (Canaan),[9] from the east and from the land of India, from various cities—khans and sultans, *mīrzās*, *mīrsofi*, *vakīls*, *vazīrs*, *sheikh ul-Islams* and sheikhs, *mullabaşıs* and mullas, *kalāntars*, meliks, head of provinces, notables and *kadḵodās* who administered districts. They gathered and continued to increase and by the time of their *bayram*[10] they had all arrived and were housed.

Each one of them presented himself at the daily *salām* of the great Khan's divan. They went in order, beginning with those who

---

[1]The correct spelling is Souqbelāğ, but there are three such places: one near Qazvīn (Šahrīyār), the other near Ray, and the last is another name for Mehābād.

[2]He belonged to the Afšār tribe.

[3]Probably Reżā Qolī Khan.

[4]'Uğūrlū Khan Zīyād Oğlī Qāǰār, son of Kalb 'Alī Khan.

[5]David II (1722-1732), the great-grandson of T'eimuraz I of Kakhet'i.

[6]MS *g* has 'Alī Qolī.

[7]Qeirāt Khan Lezgī.

[8]MSS. *a, b, c, d, e, f, v1, v2* have Mursa Qolī, Brosset has Murād Qolī.

[9]Abraham must have meant the regions of eastern Mesopotamia, which were, at times, subordinate to Iran.

[10]*Bayram* means holiday, in this case the holiday in question is *'Id ul-Fiṭr*.

had come from Ḵorāsān and ending with those from Azerbaijan and Ararat. The leaders from each city came with their notables. After the *salām* they would remain for some time in the [tent] and afterwards each would return to their own quarters.

Chapter XXIX
The Description of the Moğān Steppe and the Arax River, Where It Begins and Where It Ends

When, as noted, the notables and grandees from all the cities and provinces of Persia gathered, each was housed in a tent made of thin reeds, for it was wintertime and it rained. This large and boundless plain, called the Moğān, is wide and delightful. A good rider would hardly be able to circle it in thirty days. It is flat and even. Its elevation is higher in the west and lower in the east, hence the Arax flows from west to east.

The Arax has its source in the mountains of Garin, that is, Erzerum. It flows through Kaghzvan (Kaghzovan) and reaches Artashat[1] and Virap in the Araratian province. It gently flows by the Virap monastery and then continuing through Sharur, it reaches Astabad. Moving through the outskirts of the villages facing the monastery [of Astabad], it enters mountains and cliffs and reaches Darashamb,[2] where the river Tghmut[3] joins it. The river Tghmut is the same river [by the banks of which] the battle of Vardanank and the heroic deeds [of the Armenians] took place. Darashamb is located on the other side of Arax, towards the east and Tabrīz, for Tabrīz is three days journey from Darashamb.

---

[1]Artashat or Artaxata, the ancient capital of Armenia, was built by King Artashes (Artaxiad I) in the second century B.C. Its ruins are presently located in the Artashat region, southeast of Ējmiatsin, on the left bank of the Arax, in Armenia.

[2]A settlement and a monastery west of Julfa, close to the Alinja Çay, which flows into the right bank of the Arax in Iran. Remnants of a wooden bridge mentioned by seventeenth-century travelers are to be found there.

[3]A river which flows from the Mākū region into the Arax. The battle of Awarayr between the Persians and Armenians was fought by its banks on 26 May 451.

After Darashamb, the river passes through a mountain in the direction of Julfa (Jugha).[1] Here one encounters [the remnants of] a large and surprising bridge. This tall bridge with three bays causes amazement in all that see it. It was destroyed by Shah ʻAbbās the Great at the time when he drove away the population of Julfa. The bridge is currently not functioning and travelers from Julfa to Tabrīz cross the river by boat.

From Julfa the Arax enters a plain and flows straight for some five to six hours of travel time until it reaches the village of Dasht[2] and the town of Orduvar (Ordubad).[3] Then it once more enters rocky cliffs and inaccessible mountains, flows through the ravine of Meghri, and then passes the provinces of Chavndur[4] and Bargushat.[5]

After that the Arax reaches the Moğān Steppe, south of which is Karādāğ (Karadagh), and north of it Kap'an,[6] Karabagh, Dizak, Genjebasan province, Varanda,[7] Khachen,[8] Gandzasar, and the land of the Aghuank' (Albanians).[9]

Thus, when the Arax enters the Moğān plain it flows smoothly and moving through it a travel distance of four to five days, it reaches the Kura River and joins it at the site of the gathering of the Persians—as I have narrated. After that the waters of both rivers flow through the land of Gīlān and empty into the Caspian Sea.

---

[1] Old Julfa (in present-day Nakhichevan), on the left bank of the Arax, was a thriving commercial center until 1604, when Shah ʻAbbās transferred its Armenian merchants to his capital and settled them across the river from Isfahan in New Julfa.

[2] Present-day lower Akulis in Nakichevan.

[3] A town on the bank of the Arax in present-day Nakhichevan.

[4] A village and fort (where Armenians under Dawit' Beg resisted the Turks) in present-day Azerbaijan.

[5] Present-day Qubadli region in Azerbaijan.

[6] A main town in present-day Zangezur, Armenia.

[7] One of the five districts of Mountainous Karabagh.

[8] One of the five districts of Mountainous Karabagh.

[9] Refers to Caucasian Albania, an ancient land which stretched east of the Kura River to the Caspian Sea.

The Moğān Steppe is located in the southeast. If one puts an apple on the ground, it can be seen from far away, for there is not a single stone or even evidence of stone, on this flat plain. However, plenty of grass and rush grows on it and it is full of wild fowl and boars, which, like sheep, move in herds.

The plain is without a source of water, however. Only between Ascension and Pentecost, when the snow melts, the Arax overflows its banks and irrigates a large part of the plain. During winter there is no shortage of rain or snow, as we have witnessed. The snow, however, does not remain on the ground for more than a day, for the plain is warm, the air very humid, and it is very, very damp. Everything, therefore, gets moldy fast. In December and January green grass grows here which is sufficient for sheep and cattle. Large lambs are born and raised here, the same as in the land of Rum in the days of *khtrēlēz.*[1]It gets cold sometimes and even frosty, but it does not last long. On the banks of the Arax there are some dry spots, grottos, and a great deal of wood, which can be used for fuel.

Chapter XXX

On the Distribution of Tents to the Guests. On the Organization of the Divan. On the Rank of the Sons, Nephews, and the Khans. On the Formation and Number of the Troops, who are Always Present in the Dīvān with Their Banners. The Description of J̌azāyirčīs[2]and Their Firearms.

They housed all that had arrived in separate tents built for each of them. At sunrise, they [and their retinue] stood in their rush tents, which were situated near the quarters of the great Khan.

---

[1]Refers to *hıdrellez* (*ḵeżerlez*), the 40th day after the spring equinox (around the first week in May), which was popularly believed (in some regions) to be the beginning of summer. It coincides with the feast of St. Gregory.

[2]Infantry units armed with heavy muskets, known as *ǰazāyir*, comparable to the fussiliers.

In the second or third hour [after sunrise] the Khan would enter the *dīvānḵāne* and sit down. The *çavuşes*—there were thirty of them—stood daily before him and prayed loudly. After that, three thousand *ǰazāyirčīs*, who were the Khan's musketeers,[1]together with their commanders of a thousand,[2]entered the wood fenced area and stood in rows of two or three. They held their very large firearms in their hands. Each of the guns weighed more than fifteen *okka*.[3]They held their arms with the barrels pointing upwards. Half of each barrel was decorated with golden rings, the other half with silver rings. They leaned on the guns as if they were rods. On their heads they wore felt hats which are [like] *keçe-kalpak*. The flaps of the caps hung at both ends and on all the three thousand caps there were the words *Allah-yallah* written in three ways. Thus they stood in compact rows right next to each other, scaring those who looked at them.

By the side of the Khan, near him, stood his brother, Ebrāhīm Khan. Next stood the eldest son of the Khan, Reżā Qolī Khan, and then the nephew [of the Khan] Mortażā Qolī Khan, who was younger. Next to him stood the younger son of the great Khan, Moḥammad 'Alī Khan, [who was] younger still, and farther stood other khans according to their rank and merit.

On the other side there was a circle with two rows: In one row stood *chandauls*[4]who wore *jghas*[5]with feathers, which seemed to be the real feathers of a cock.

In the second [row] stood the *nasaqčīs*; whose commander had three feathers in his cap, two on each side and one in the middle.

Most of the troops had stands resembling those [used] for arrows. They were made of copper or silver and were gilded. They

---

[1]The text has *tüfenkçi*.

[2] The *minbaşı*.

[3]MS *c* has 55.

[4]Refers to *čandāvul*, or the rear guard.

[5]The term is *ǰiğā* or *ǰeğe (ǰeqe)*, which was a plume or tuft of feathers worn by princes or officers of high rank in shape of a crest. It was also an adornment worn by champions and special guards. Although the *čandāvuls* had feathers on their headgear, it was not the same as the *ǰiğā* worn by princes.

had three or four arrow-like notches, which were made of feathers measuring a span. They always have Damascus [steel] axes in their hands, with silver plated handles. The duty of the *čandāvuls* is to guard the roads, like a *bostançı-başı*.[1] They check the roads, ravines, and gullies. They also guard the outside of the camp at night. If the Khan wishes to execute anyone, the person is handed to them [the *čandāvuls*] and they kill him on his orders.

The duties of the *nasaqčīs* are to communicate orders to the troops during battle, to prohibit,[2] that is, to forbid that which is unlawful,[3] and to lead the troops to the place of battle. If anyone tries to flee, they are to kill him. The Khan sends them when he wishes to summon someone. They are also sent to faraway places as ruthless executioners, for they immediately carry out their orders. They perform the duty of camp guards day and night. They rule over thieves and bandits, and if thieves steal anything from the camp, the owners of the goods demand it from the *nasaqčīs* and get them.

In addition to these, there are also heralds,[4] who daily, proclaim and announce to the troops that which is ordered by the great Khan. They do the same during battle.

Moreover, the Khan has 6,000 sentinels,[5] who tie a white band to their hats. The hats cannot be seen. All that is visible is the white band tied around it. They are also armed with guns. They take turn guarding the quarters of the Khan day and night in groups of 2,000, which rotate every three days. [Altogether] there were three hundred *čandāvuls*, three hundred *nasaqčīs*,[6] and three hundred

---

[1]The *bostançıs* guarded roadways and canals. Their commander was the head of the imperial guard and was charged with the execution of grandees.

[2]The text has *ghadagha* (*qadağan*), which has a variety of meanings depending on its spelling (q or ğ) such as to command, to prohibit, to threaten with punishment, or to cease.

[3]The text has *yasakh* (*yasak*).

[4]The text has *jarchi* (*ǰārǰī, ǰārčī*).

[5]The text has *kešīkčī*.

[6]MS *d* is missing the second 300.

eliaghaǰlīs.[1] The *elāğāǰlīs*,[2] the children of khans or brothers of khans, were always on duty before the Khan. If the Khan got angry with someone and ordered that he were to be beaten, they would beat him. They would throw him on the ground and five or six *elāğāǰlīs* would stand over him and beat him mercilessly until the Khan would say, "Enough! Release him!"

Chapter XXXI
On How They Once Again Pitched the Great Tent and On the Salām on the Day of `Arif[3]

The day of *Ramadhan-bayram*[4] approached and the Khan once again ordered that the great tent be set up, for after the first time they took it apart after three days and had hidden it.

On the day of *'arif* the tent was once more made ready on the eastern side of the Khan's quarters.

On the day of *'arif*, when all went for *salām* early in the morning, half an hour after sunrise, the mighty, wise, and genius-like Khan came out of his quarters and on the eastern side of the wooden fence he stood with his face northward.

His brother Ebrāhīm Khan stood next to him on the left. Behind the brother stood the eldest son [of the Khan] Reżā Qoli Khan. The Khan's nephew, Mortażā Qolī Khan, who was younger than the oldest son [of the Khan], stood behind the eldest son; the youngest son Moḥammad 'Alī Khan, behind the nephew, for he was

---

[1]The correct term is *elāğāǰlī*, who were also called *čūbdārān* (one who is armed with a cudgel) or *ḵānzādegān* (sons of khans). MSS. *d* and *f* have the last 300 inserted by another hand.

[2]MS d has " the 300 *eliaghaj*"

[3]The day before the end of *Ramadhan*. *Ramadhan* began on 4 (15 N.S.) January 1736.

[4]Abraham uses *bayram* for a number of different Muslim holidays. In this case he once again means *'Id ul-Fiṭr*, the celebration to mark the end of *Ramadhan*, the month of fasting for Muslims, which occurs on the 9th month of the Muslim calendar. The holiday is on the first day of the 10th month (*Shawwal*). It occurred on 3 (14 N.S.) February 1736.

younger than the nephew. The other khans stood according to their rank and merit.

At some distance stood the 3,000 *ǰazāyirčīs*, holding their huge guns in their hands. The *amasha*[1] *kešīkčīs* stood at the other side of the *ǰazāyirčīs*, holding regular guns in their hands. Facing them stood the *çavuş*, and closer yet the *čandāvuls* and the *nasaqčīs*. Straight in front of them stood the *elāǧāǰlīs*, who were the sons and the brothers of khans.

The great Khan ordered that camels be brought and be forced to fight each other in his presence. Following the camel fight they ordered wrestlers, who were *pahlavāns*,[2] to wrestle each other.

They then ordered that everyone who was present pass before him [the Khan] and go through the *salām* ceremony as they had done the day before and the day before that. Thus the men from various cities walked one after the other in front of him [the Khan] and silently bowed and greeted him. After the conclusion of the *salām* everyone returned to his quarters.

Chapter XXXII
On How They Prepared and Seated the Invited Guests. On How They Had to Walk in a Procession to the Big Tent and Stand Before the Khan

The next day, which was their big *bayram*, we gathered outside the residence of the great Khan early in the morning, where we waited and rested under rush awnings, in huts prepared for us. For when we were returning to our quarters the day before--the day of *'arif*--I asked the *kalāntar* and the melik, "Tomorrow is *bayram*. What time should we go for the *salām*? Is it necessary to go or not? They answered, "Yes we shall go, for such is the custom. We should go tomorrow the same time as we have done every day." I said, "That is not so. For in Turkey, in the country

---

[1]The word is *hamīše* or constant/permanent guard.

[2]A champion, a strong athlete, a wrestler, or a brave warrior.

of Rum, and in Constantinople, the *salām* and prayer [of the *bayram*] is performed early in the morning, before sunrise. The nobles go to the royal palace for the *salām*, and then they all gather and go to prayer.[1] After that, they gather and once again congratulate [the ruler] on the *bayram* and then they depart. We should, therefore, go to our cabins [and retire] earlier, an hour before sunset, for they [officials of the Khan] may wish to organize the *salām* earlier." They accepted my suggestion and said, "Good! We shall do so."

Therefore, very early, prior to sunrise, we went to the place that was reserved for us [and rested under the awning]. The *nasaqčīs* greeted us kindly and respectfully seated us.

Soon after the envoy from Moscow[2] arrived. They greeted him in the same fashion and seated him in another section.

Soon after many people arrived and gathered in that place: khans, sultans, *mīrzās*, *mīrsofis*, *kalāntars*, meliks, *mullah-başıs*, mullahs, *kadḵodās*, other notables, heads of one thousand men (*mīn-bşıs*), heads of one hundred men (*yüz-başıs*) heads of fifty men (*elli-başıs*),[3] heads of ten men (*on-başıs*), *ǰazayirčīs*, *hamīše kešikčīs*, *čandāvuls*, *nasaqčīs*, *ḵānzādehs* (sons of khans) or *elāğāǰlīs*, and many others. There were almost not enough places for all of them.

The 3,000 *ǰazayirčīs* formed two rows in front of the wooden fence of the Khan's residence. Each row was the same length and was as long, or even longer, as the flight of an arrow. The Ottomans call such rows *alay*.[4] They carried their big guns in their hands.

Through these rows they escorted the Ottoman envoy, Ganǰ 'Alī Pasha, and took him to the big tent before anyone else. After that they escorted the Russian envoy to the tent.

---

[1] The text has *namāz*.

[2] Ivan Petrovich Kalushkin was the Russian ambassador to the Persian court from 1735 to 1742.

[3] MS *f* has the *elli-başı* inserted by another hand.

[4] Troops in line during a procession or a ceremony.

Each one of us invited guests were in turn taken and seated in his place, for places were prepared for all of us on separate long benches [under a long awning]. On the Khan's order they called each one individually and escorted him to his designated place. The wise Khan had ordered the names of those invited to be recorded on paper in order [of importance]. Thus accordingly, they would mark the list and escort the person from his hut to his allotted place.

The procedure was followed again and again so that each person would know and remember his place, who was above him and who was below him, so that they would not make mistakes or be confused. Thus they would go in order to the big tent, humble, quiet, and steady. Thus they would not rush when they sat or got up, but would rise and descend sensibly and with decorum.

After that, all of us who were invited, whose name was on the list, sat for about half an hour. There were only khans and no one else, and I—among the khans. Each one carefully noted and remembered his place. We were silent and awaited to be summoned to the other [big] tent.

Chapter XXXIII

On the Salām of the Day of Bayram. On the Ceremonies and Honors. On How the Great Khan Honored the Khans and I with Sweet Şerbet,[1] Rosewater, and Fragrances

Then by the order of the great Khan and the *ḵānzādehs*, who were the *elāğāǰlīs*, they came and invited us to the other tent. Following the order that they had taught us, we moved one by one, entered through the wooden fence, and reached the big tent.

We removed our shoes outside the tent, and entered with fear and reverence. We stood in the middle, bowed our heads, saluted him, congratulated him on the *bayram*, and dispersed to the various

[1]Sherbet, *šarbat* in Persian, water mixed with sweetened fruit or herb syrup.

corners of the long tent, sitting on our knees contemplating silently.

The Khan sat in the tent in the place of prominence, which resembled a small cell. There were three special places at the end of the tent, each covered with a net[1] resembling a small tent with a door-like partition covered by a curtain. In one of these sat the Khan facing and observing us all, for his curtain was lifted.

On the right of the great Khan, in those small separate places, sat the Ottoman envoy, Ganǰ ʻAlī Pasha, and below him seven or eight khans and the *vālī* (viceroy) of Tiflis, who was his [the Khan's] brother-in-law and who was above me. They call him the *vālī*, for alone can wear the *ǰeqe*,[2] as the deputy of the shah. The *vālī* is ranked higher than the khans and this *vālī* ruled over Tiflis and the Khanate of Kakhetʻi.[3]

My seat was situated below his.

Below me were 45 khans, as the khan of Erevan, Moḥammad Qolī, later told the *kalāntar* and the melik of Erevan. It was he who recalled this, for I was so delighted and shocked that my mind could not comprehend its significance.

Similarly, on the left, across from us sat: first, the Khan's brother, Ebrāhīm Khan, then the Khan's eldest son Reżā Qolī Khan, and further from him sat the son of Ebrahim, ʻAlī Qolī Beg. Below him sat the youngest son of the Khan, Mortażā Qolī Mīrzā. Below them sat the Russian envoy.[4] Further, just as on our side, sat khans and other elders in order. Separate from the envoys and the

---

[1]Text has *jibinlukh*, the correct word is *cibinlik*, which is a mosquito net.

[2]The *ǰeqe* in this case had plumes in shape of a crest.

[3]He was Tʻeimuraz II, the ruler of Kakhetʻi (part of eastern Georgia) who married Tʻamar, daughter of Wakhtang VI, ruler of Kʻartʻli. His son Erekle II (d. 1798) accompanied Nāder (probably as a hostage) on his Indian campaign. Both father and son were elevated to the posts of *vālī*, in 1744, after aiding Nāder in his last Turkish campaign. Following Nāder's death, as well as the death of his maternal grandfather, Erekle united the kingdoms of Kʻartʻli and Kakhetʻi (1762) and became the sole ruler of all of eastern Georgia. The dynastic struggles in Iran, enabled Erekle to become the most powerful ruler in Transcaucasia during the second half of the 18th century.

[4]The text has the Turkish term, *elçi*.

khans sat the *mīrzās* who were subject to the khans, and [a few] others. No one else sat there. Although I in my fear and reverence did not count, it seems that there were some 100 persons in that [select] gathering maybe a little more or a little less.

The rest of the notables and the *mīn-başıs*, *yüz-başıs*, *on-başıs*, and *mīrzās* stood behind us, who were seated. In the four[1] corners of the tent, in linen measuring two spans high and in the shape of railings, or as the Ottomans say, *parmaklık*,[2] was a separate place which was one and a half *ḥalebi* wide, resembling a narrow road covered with carpets. On it were those who stood, while we, were on the other side of the railing and sat in front of those who stood.

In the middle of the tent, on both sides of the columns, were spread two valuable tablecloths. On the right side of the tablecloths, on our side, stood three large golden bowls,[3] resembling the sherbet bowls that stand on the tablecloths in Istanbul, and in the land of the Greeks. In addition there were three flagons,[4] that is decanters,[5] but somewhat flatter. In each decanter they mixed five or six *okka* of water. There were also three golden trays,[6] which were one and half spans[7] wide and on each of them up to seven golden wineglasses, resembling golden cupolas. They stood on golden plates, which were placed on golden trays. The plates stood lightly on long legs. Golden cups were placed between the plates.

There were also two large golden censers, each one of which weighed approximately 1,000 *dirhams* or maybe even more. On them hung short chains. Each one had four chain-pattern edgings[8] without bells. The length of the chain was half of that of our censers. Above the chain there was a handle resembling the handle of

---

[1] MS *g* has 24.

[2] Translates as railing or banister.

[3] The text has *bād* (*a form of bādeh*).

[4] The text has *tung* (*tange*) which is a short-neck vessel with a narrow mouth.

[5] The text has *surakh*, which is actually *ṣurāhi* or a long-necked flask.

[6] MSS. *f*, *v1* do not state "three."

[7] The text has *t'iz*, which is a length of a palm of a hand.

[8] The text has *zenjelov*, which is actually *zencire* (*zanǰīr*).

a pail or a lantern.[1] The chains were fastened to these handles, two on one side and two on the other. The same number and shape were on the left side—in silver.

The large bowls were filled with sweet sherbet. On top of the sherbet swam basil (*reyḥān*) seeds. Also on the right were three golden trays, one and a half *ḥalebi* wide, and three silver ones on the left. On them were placed sugar cones, which resembled small heads of Venetian sugar. They began to serve the invited guests, starting with the mighty Khan. They served rosewater poured in golden dishes to both groups. After that they served everyone on both sides from silver dishes.

After that they brought the golden censers and began to burn fragrant incense. They did not disperse the incense close to the face as we do, but moved it to the right and left. They passed through everyone and burned it in all four sides. Following the two golden censers they brought two silver ones. The golden ones were taken to the eastern and southern side [of the tent], while the silver ones to the western and northern side.

While they were burning the incense throughout the tent, servants brought the sherbet in golden cups, which sat on circular holders inside plates. They poured the sherbet from the flagons into the seven[2] cups and holding the plate in the left hand and the cup in the right, they served those seated. When the sherbet was consumed they poured some more from the flagons, that is from the decanters. If the sherbet in the decanter was empty they poured more from the bowls into the empty decanter, until everyone who sat in the tent had drunk. After that they served those standing behind us in the tent--grandees, commanders, *mīrzās*, and the many governors and provincial chiefs. They received their sherbet in silver cups.

After that they brought adult and young singers and sweet-voiced children, who wore stoles which resembled those worn by our churchmen. The stoles were put around the necks of the chil-

[1] The text has *fener* (*fanār*).

[2] MS *a*, has "big" instead of "seven."

dren and covered both their hands by over two spans. The corners hung on their hands. There were bells attached to their feet. They danced in front of the great Khan and the great multitude. There were twenty-two of them. Some of the musicians sat in front of the Khan with their *santūrs,*[1] *tambūras,*[2] *kamānças,*[3] *kanuns,*[4] and other musical instruments. They played and made each instruments make its own appropriate sounds. The dancers sang while dancing. They sang only one tune and did not alter their style. Although the dancers sang one melody, the audience sang each in his own way.

The singers and dancers continued to sing and dance for one hour, while the servants passed the censers around. After that the gathering ended and each person went to his quarters. However, I was invited by the son of Askhal Bek of Tiflis, whose name was Aqā [Bek], and who was the *kalāntar* and melik of Tiflis and was born in those parts, to his tent to honor me together with our *kalāntar*, melik, princes, *kadḵodās* of Erevan, Astabad, Nakhichevan, and Goght‘. In front of his tent, where we were sitting by the table, at a distance of some two stone-throws away, a tightrope walker[5] performed [acrobatics] on a rope.

In the evening we rose and went to the tent of the *mīrzās* of Erevan and congratulated them on the *bayram.* We then returned to our quarters, praising and glorifying God, Who holds the heart of kings in His Hand.[6] He shows favors to those He wishes and shows wrath on those He wishes.

---

[1]A string instrument consisting of a fret board with numerous strings, all running the length of a flat shallow resonator and played by striking the strings with thin curved wooden hammers.

[2]A *tambur* is a small drum as well as a special type of Persian lute played by plucking. Although Abraham does not mention which instrument, the lute is more probable.

[3]A small string instrument resembling a cantaloupe-shaped viola.

[4]A zither-like instrument with many strings.

[5]The text has *jānbāz*, literally "one who risks his life."

[6]Refers to *Proverbs*, 21.1 "The king's heart is a stream of water in the hand of the Lord; he turns it wherever he will."

Chapter XXXIV

On How On the Second Day of Bayram They Took Us to the Field Outside the Camp and Ordered Us to Confer with Each Other and to Elect Someone, who Could Rule the Persian State and Become the Ruler Over All.

On the second day of *bayram* we once again went to the *salām*. At the third hour [after sunrise] they invited us to an open field, at a distance of one day's march from the residence of the great Khan. They ordered that each khan, together with his followers, separate themselves from others and reflect.

They sat in groups of 50-100 men, some more, some less.

They began to reflect and to ask each other, "Why have they summoned us? Why have they gathered us together here? What do they wish to ask us?"

Then, seven men came from the great Khan. They were: Mīrzā Zakī,[1] Mīrzā Mahdī,[2] a khan whom they called Valī Ṭahmāsp,[3] the *ma'yār-başı* of Isfahan, that is the *ṣāḥeb-e 'ayār*,[4] 'Abd ol-Qadīm Mīrzā of Kāšān, 'Alī Akbar Mīrzā of Ḵorāsān, and the *ṣanduqdār*[5] of the great Khan.

They stood in one place and ordered the *ǰārčīs* and *nasaqčīs* to invite the people of each land to come before them separately. Each group, together with their khans, *kalāntars*, meliks, *kadḵodās*, *mīrzās* and *ẓābets* [were taken to them]. They placed other *ǰarčīs* and *nasaqčīs* around themselves [in a circle]. They then brought each group into the circle and the above [seven] men would address those men in each group who were known to and respected by their followers, reading the following order, "The great Khan has decreed that you go and confer with each other.

---

[1]Refers To Mīrzā Zakī Nadīm from Mašhad, a close advisor of Nāder.

[2]Mīrzā Mahdī was the head of the scribes, later court historian, see bibliography.

[3]Refers to Ṭahmāsp Khan J̌alāyer, who actually led this delegation.

[4]Probably Ḥasan 'Alī Khan; he was in charge of the weight and standards of the coins of the realm.

[5]The treasurer, controller of privy purse.

Decide whom you wish to rule over you and the country. Whom do you elect to keep peace and tranquility in the land? For he [the Khan] is old and weary from years of fighting. With the help of God he has rid Persia of its enemies. He has crushed and driven them out of the country. The land is now pacified. He wishes to leave for K̲orāsān, to settle down in his castle, and to pray for himself and for you. Therefore, confer until the ninth hour and at the ninth hour gather here again and individually express your opinion and wish and we shall inform the Khan of your reply.

Chapter XXXV
On How We Gathered, Conferred, and Returned Early to the Same Place and Begged that He Rule Over Persia. How He Demanded Three Conditions

We went and conferred until the eighth hour and then we returned to the same place. Fearing that we would be suspected of vacillating, we rushed and returned an hour earlier. Once again, the same individuals—seven men—whom we have mentioned, came and stood before us, just as they did the morning before. They called us once more and inquired our answer. They found out that we were all of the same opinion and will. They began asking us from the eighth hour and barely finished by sunset. They then ordered, "Go and come back early in the morning."

The next day, which was the third day[1] of *bayram*, Thursday, 5 February, we went very early to the places allocated to us before [near the residence of the Khan] and sat down. After three hours they took us from here again to the plain and ordered that each khan and his grandees and *kadk̲odās* separate themselves. We thus sat separate from each other on the bare ground covered with grass.

Those gathered began to talk, listen, or confer. From among our group they chose some Persians and asked them to respond to the questions put to them. From the Armenians only the *kalāntar*, the

---

[1]*Bayram* was on 3 February.

melik, and I were permitted to be spokesmen. Each group selected their own spokesmen, including those from Azerbaijan, Georgia, and all other regions, nominated men who would answer any questions posed by the seven men.

They then once again stood in a great circle, as they had done yesterday, and the day before. Inside the circle stood the same seven men. The Vakīl Ṭahmāsp began to speak and said, "Listen you khans, sultans, begs, *āqās*, the distinguished[1] caliph of the Armenians, *kadḵodās*, notables, and all of you who have arrived from afar and near. Here is the will of the great Khan, "Since you will not let me go and do not wish that I retire to my abode and rest there, and since you will not leave my banner, I demand from you these three conditions:

First, if after some time a son or relative of the shah appears or takes the field, you will not join him, will not aid[2] him, and will not accept him.

Second, do not utter the curses and the derogatory words, which you have uttered against 'Omar ('Umar) and 'Osmān ('Uthman).[3] Do not on the day of *nowruz-bayram*[4] scratch and bloody your faces in the name of Ḥasan and Ḥosein, but in accordance with this agreement stand firm in your promise [not to do so]. For it is because of this obnoxious behavior that streams of blood have flowed between the two people who read the Qur'an—between two states—Iran and Turkey—and have caused the imprisonment of many. Henceforth such confusion and animosity shall cease between us. After all we have the same prophet and the same Qur'an, and the same prayer (*namāz*). Because the Ottomans pray with their hands placed on their heart, while we pray with our

[1]The text has *sar-afrāz*, a Persian term meaning exalted, glorious, eminent, and distinguished.

[2]The text has the Persian word *komak.*

[3]Refers to the split between the Sunni and the Shi'i regarding the caliphate and the leadership of the Muslim world.

[4]Abraham means the first month of the Muslim calendar, *Muḥarram*, during which (9th or 10th day) the martyrdom of Imam Ḥosein (*'āšūrā*) is reenacted in passion plays (*ta'zīya*) by the Shi'is.

hands freely facing down--let it be so. Let them follow their rite and we ours and thus cease abusing each other. When [pilgrims] from Persia travel to the *Ka'ba*,[1] they should not be offended and no one should demand more from them, but accept them as their own *ḥājjīs* and their own brothers. Since one can pray from all four sides in the *Ka'ba*, you can pray from whatever side you wish.[2] Do not violate the conditions of this agreement.

Third, since it is your wish that I rule over you, then after my death do not commit evil deeds against my clan and my children, but remain forever obedient. Affirm to these three demands, your oaths, your signatures, and your seals and return them to me. What do you say? Do you accept or not?" They immediately read the *fatwa*[3] and let us go.

Chapter XXXVI

On How the Valīne'mat Summoned the Khans and Refused to Accept the Throne. On How the Khans Entreated Him not to Abandon Them and the Country

On Friday early in the morning, we went to the *salām* and in the fifth[4] hour they took us to him. We passed in order in front of him, bowing our heads and saluted him. Upon exiting we went to the places prepared for our rest. The *ǰazāyirčīs* also dispersed after the *salām*. The *Valīn'emat* invited the khans to lunch.

He then spoke a long time with them and found various reasons to refuse the crown saying, "Elect someone else from among yourselves, a man who could rule you and the country. Leave me in

---

[1]The holiest shrine of the Muslims, located in the city of Mecca, the site of an annual pilgrimage, the *ḥaǰǰ*.

[2]It implies that they can continue to follow the Twelfth Imam, Imam J̌a'far al-Sadeq, who was descended from the Prophet as the head of their sect or *ṭarīqa* (path).

[3]A judicial decree usually pronounced by a *mufti* (magistrate).

[4]MSS. *f, v1* have third hour.

peace. Let me go to my fortress in K̲orāsān and seek solitude. For I have no more strength to battle and drive out enemies."

He refused many times. But the khans insisted, begged, flattered, implored, and persuaded him not to abandon them or the country.

Answering them, the shrewd *Valīne'mat* said, "You are saying this, but I know that among you there are many who are not satisfied with me. They have the right, for I took the belongings from many, killed many, destroyed many, and took lots of gold and silver from many. I turned many places into ruins. I terrorized and ravaged the land. Enough evil deeds! Let the people henceforth be free from such oppression.

The khans responded by saying, "That which you state is true, but it was necessary to do so to achieve your lofty position and to command the troops. If you were not so steadfast in all things, how could you accomplish so many great deeds? We, therefore, ask you once more, to do as you have done, for God has given you the power to rule over the land. Everyone is indebted to you and shall obey your every command. Those who dare to defy you deserve to be judged and condemned. Let those who obey your orders be honored and given *k̲al'ats*. For otherwise it will not be possible to rule the country."

He approved these statements and accepted the crown. They once again read the *fatwa* and I whispered the prayer, "Father I have sinned [*Hayr Meghayn*]." Then they let us go to our quarters.

Chapter XXXVII

On How They Affixed the Agreement with Seals. On How They Implored Him to Accept the Crown and on the Conditions Which He Asked to be Included in the Agreement. On How He Entrusted Me to the Khan of Erevan

They then wrote a long agreement, which was two spans wide. After they revised and corrected it again and again, the agreement conformed to [his] wishes. They then asked those present to affix their seals to it. The khans, sultans, *mīrzās*, *mīrsofīs*, *mīn-başıs*, *yüz-başıs*, *kalāntars*, meliks, notables,[1] *āqās*, *sheikh ul-Islam*, and judges,[2] both Persians and Armenians, of each city affixed their seals to the document. They started with those from K̲orāsān, Herāt, Mašhad, Māzandarān, and thus in order reached the men from Azerbaijan.[3]

When their turn came, they invited those from Ararat to affix their seals to the agreement. They barely managed to finish the job in three days. We all affixed our seals, especially those, who we mentioned above in chapter thirty-five, the ones who had acted as spokesmen, and the seven [men] who had presented the conditions.[4]

When all of this was completed, we once again began to go daily at the third hour, filed in order, and saluted him as we had done before.

On 10 February, when we went to salute him, he called us [the Armenians] to his presence and said. "Caliph, caliph!"[5] I answered, "*Bali* (yes), my *Valīn'emat*,"[6] for the Persians say *bali*[7] instead of *buyur*.[8]

The mightiest *Valīne'mat* said, "Do you know, or is it unknown to you that I have well taken care of your affairs?"[9]

I replied, "It is your will, you most august one. Let it be blessed."[10]

---

[1]The text has *a'yān*.

[2]The text has *qāẓī* (*qadhi*).

[3]A damaged copy containing 42 (the rest have been torn) square, rectangular and oval seals (most of them undecipherable) exists; facsimile in M. Qodūsī, *Nāder-nāme* (Mašhad, 1960), pp. 303-304.

[4]They signed a muster-roll or *maḥẓar-nāme* (also called *vas̲īqe-nāme)*

[5]The text has *Khalifay, Khalifay*.

[6]The text has *Bali Vēlinemat'in*.

[7]Pronounced *balé* and translates as *yes*.

[8]Used in respectful speech, such as "command me," "what is your wish."

[9]The text is in Turkish written in Armenian letters as follows: *Bildin khabardar san sizē bēk dik'dim*.

[10]The text is in Turkish written in Armenian letters: *Ikhtiar sēnin dir. Shefk'et'lum mubarak' olsun.*

Right then Pīr Moḥammad Khan of Herāt came running and stood before him [the Khan] with his hands on his heart.

The *Valīne‘mat* stated, “This khan—is Pīr Moḥammad of Herāt. He is a good man. He treats people well. He has to treat you well too and you now have to serve him well, as you have served me. He is yet uninformed and you have to inform him. I now appoint you [Abraham] the master over all the [Armenian] *āqās* of Erevan. I trust you. If any illegal act takes place, you, caliph, have to go to your *beg*. If he does not listen to you, then you will go to Ebrāhīm Khan of Tabrīz, and if Ebrāhīm Khan does not resolve the problem, you have the right to come directly to me.”[1]

He then turned to the khan and said, “Pīr Moḥammad Khan, do you see these people? These are my people. This caliph is a very good man. Üç-Kilisa is a good place. I now entrust them to you. Let him not complain about you. Listen to him, treat him kindly and respect him. He is an honorable and loyal man. He is concerned about the land, the *ra‘yat*, and the *dīvān*. This *kalāntar* [of the Armenians] has also served me well. He is one of the *āqās* of Erevan and has performed his duties well.”[2]

[1]The text is in Turkish written in Armenian letters: *Ishday bu khan, dur Pir Mehmed Khan, Herat‘ khani. Yakhshi kishi dur, yakhshi yolay gēdup‘ dur. Sizin ilēndē yakhshi yola kēt‘mēk‘ kērēk‘ dur. Indi sizdē onay yakhshi ghulukh ēylēmēk kerēk suz, nēt‘ēkin ozumay ēylēdiniz. Indi oghu nabalat‘ dur, sez kearak‘ ozuna khabar verēsuz. Indi sani Ērewan aghalarun hamisinum usdinay aghay et‘misham. Sanday ekhdibarum var dur. Hargiz bir nashari ish olsay, bēginizay dēyēsun. Ghulakh ki asmasay Tarvizē Ibrahim Khanay arz ēylēmēk kērēk sun. Ochagh ki Ibrahim Khan bashay ap‘armasun, san Ghalifay, murakhasun ozun garak‘ manay arz ēylēyēsun.*

[2]The text is in Turkish written in Armenian letters: *Pir Mahmad Khan, bu k‘ishilaru gorur san. Bunlar manum dur. Bu khalifay chok yakhshi kishi dur. Uck‘ilisay bir yakhchi er dur. Indi sanay t‘apshuriram, kērēk‘ nēdēsay gulak‘ asasan, yakhshi mehrabanlukh ēylasan, khat‘rn sakhlayasan. Bir ēhdibarlu k‘ishi dur olk‘eaeay, rahat‘ay vē divanay mughiat‘ oluf dur. Bu kalant‘ar, da yakhshi ghulukh ēylēab dur. Bu Ērewann aghznay kēn dur. Yakhchi eyola gēdup‘ dur.*

About Melik Mkrtum he stated, "And this melik is the brother of the former old melik. He has also served me well."[1]

About Melik Hakopjan he said, "And this melik was in the fortress with the Turks [during the Turkish occupation]. He also served me well. I now entrust these people to you. They are my people. Do not burden them with orders. You shall consult the caliph and these people regarding all matters [concerning Armenians]. Do not trust the *kızılbaş* and the *āqā* of Erevan. Put your trust in them. I have made you [the Armenians secular leaders] superior to the *āqā* of Erevan. You [the Armenians] are responsible for the tranquility of that province. You have to be concerned about its well-being."[2]

He then added, " Go. If you [Armenians] have any needs, projects, or petitions take them to Mīrzā Mo'men[3] or Mīrzā Mahdī. Let them see to it and make out *raqams*,[4] for I have to leave all of you soon."[5]

We were then permitted to leave and thanked him. Praising the Lord we went to our quarters with great happiness and pride.

---

[1]The text is in Turkish written in Armenian letters: *Bu mēlik'da o azalk'i k'ohnay mēlik'in gardashi dur. Buday yakhshi ghulugh ēylēib dur.*

[2]The text is in Turkish written in Armenian letters: *Bu mēlik' day ghalay day idi osmanlu ichinday, onēnday ghulukhi manay et'ēshmish dur. Imdi bu k'ishilari sanay t'apshirmisham banum durlar. Kērēk bunlarun sozindan chkhmayasan. Hēr zadi maslahat' khalifayilan munlarilan ēylēsan. Ghzlbashlaray Ērewan aghalarênay ēhdibar ēylēmēyēsn. Ēhdibarun munlaray olsun. Szi Ērewanun aghalarên uzarinay agay ēt'misham. Vilayēt'i rahat'i ozunuzdun biliram. Kērakdur k'i avadanlêghnay chalêshasêz.*

[3]Mīrzā Mo'men Khan Abīvardī, one of the *monšī* (scribes) of Nāder.

[4]*Raqam* was an official order, a writ. Abraham uses it in the same context as *farman* (*ferman*) which was a royal edict.

[5]The text is in Turkish written in Armenian letters: *Gēdn nēt'ēk'i ishinz var, maslahat'ênz var, arzayênz var, ap'arên mirzay Mominay, Mirzay Mēht'iē hami ishinzi ghayirsunlar, rakhamlarnzi eazsunlar, ki sizi eakhunday murakhas ēdērum.*

Chapter XXXVIII

On the Distribution of the K̲al'ats First in the Presence of the Valīne'mat to the Famous Khans, and Then to the Others by the Ṣanduqdār. On His Sending a K̲al'at to My Quarters

After that, on 10 February, they began to distribute *k̲ila'*, that is *k̲al'ats*. First, to his brother, whom he designated the governor and sardār—that is *sar'askar*, of the land of Atrpatakan, which in Persian is called Adrbejan (Azerbaijan). He entrusted to him Nakhichevan, Erevan and the entire Ararat region and Georgia, making him a *beglarbegī*—the commander, master, and chief over all other khans.

He then granted *k̲al'at* to Bābā Khan and ordered him to leave for K̲orāsān and Herāt in place of Pīr Moḥammad Khan.

He gave [the command] of Erevan to Pīr Moḥammad Khan and granted him *k̲al'at*.

He thus distributed *k̲al'ats* and instructions to all the khans in order of their rank and worth and gave them leave.

They then began to distribute *k̲al'ats* to other notables.

He [Nāder] presented *k̲al'ats* to the khans in his presence. They consisted of coats[1] of satin made of golden thread, trimmed with fur, and *gabas*[2] made of golden thread, valuable Circassian[3] girdles, each one of which cost three, four, or five *tomāns*. They also received a silk kerchief,[4] with which they fastened their caps.

For prior to this he had introduced a new form of headgear: the top of the cap was cross-like and had four corners; they were called *Tahmazi*.

He and everyone else wore this headgear.

---

[1]The text has *k'urdik*, which is *kyurdeki* "a kind of frock-coat with short sleeves." Appears in Russian as *kurtka* "man's jacket."

[2]The correct spelling is *qabā*, which was a long tunic or gown open in front and worn by men of position; not to be confused with *'abā,* an overcoat of inferior material worn by dervishes.

[3]The text has *Charkaz*, a variation of *Cherkes*, a tribe living in northern Caucasus. It also means a thin worsted fabric.

[4]The text has *mendil.*

He ordered the *bazrgan-başı*,[1] Ḥājjī Ḥosein, who was from Kāšān, to distribute the other *ḵal'ats*, according to rank and merit. He distributed them, but in a different way. First, he ordered that they record and read in his presence the names of each man who was elected from each city and who was among those who had affixed his seal to the agreement. Then [following each name] he would say, "Give that man *ḵal'at*, worth this many *tomāns*, and to this one, *ḵal'at* worth another sum."

First he made a list,[2] that is a *daftar* (notebook), and then according to names listed in that *daftar*, the *ṣanduqdār*, that is *bazrgan-başı*, distributed rewards and *ḵal'ats*. He began with those from the depths of Ḵorāsān and ended with those from the eastern regions.[3] Each khan was given one coat, one tunic, one girdle, and one kerchief, all with golden thread. The *mīrzās*, other notables, and main administrators of provinces were given one tunic, one girdle, and one kerchief, also of golden thread.[4]

To those from the eastern and far away provinces he gave one captive each. For they had taken 7,000 prisoners[5] from Georgia—a mixed group of Armenians and Georgians. Half of them were thus distributed, some were given women, others, men, and others, boys. The *kadḵodās* and *āqās* received one *tomān*[6] each for expenses until it came the turn of those from Azerbaijan. They were rewarded the same as noted above (gifts). After that came the turn of Erevan and Ararat. They were given the same (gifts) but no captives.[7]

---

[1]*Bazrgan* (*bazargan*)-*başı* means the head of merchants, but Ḥājjī Ḥosein was the keeper of the privy-purse (*ṣanduqdār*) as well.

[2]The text has *siahi*, which is *siyaha*.

[3]Since Ḵorāsān and Herāt are in the eastern most regions of Persia, Abraham must have meant the eastern regions as viewed from his perspective (Constantinople), hence the regions of Kurdistan, Mesopotamia, and Eastern Anatolia.

[4]The *Kondak* states that Nāder had ordered 1,000 *ḵal'ats* for the occasion.

[5]Although MSS. *a, b, c, d, e, f, , v1, v2* have 700,000, the only possible accurate number (7,000) appears in MS *g*.

[6]MSS. *f, v1* do not have "one toman."

[7]The prisoners were Christians who had lived in close proximity of the Erevan region. They would find it easy to escape and return to their homes.

On Saturday, 14 February, on the Feast of St. Sargis, the [Armenian] notables of Erevan and Nakhichevan were given *k̲al'ats*. He [probably Nāder] ordered that they bring my *k̲al'at* to my quarters first, which was half-an-hour travel from the camp and the residence of the *Valīne'mat*. Together with my *k̲al'at*, they also sent the *k̲al'at* of the *kalāntar*.

My *k̲al'at* consisted of a golden threaded tunic, a coat woven with golden thread, a heavy Circassian girdle, a superb kerchief of black color, with a white braiding, a finger wide, running through the entire side. The ends of the kerchief were woven with Indian cotton and amazed whoever saw it. They twisted this kerchief on my cowl, as if it was a fillet. The knot was, according to Persian custom, on the left side. It was in the shape of a half-opened fan[1] and resembled a flower.

They sent the *kalāntar* one tunic, one Circassian girdle, and one kerchief. But my *k̲al'at* was rare and very expensive.

Chapter XXXIX

On How, Robed in Our K̲al'ats, We Saluted, Congratulated, and Thanked Him. On How They Organized a Prayer. On How the Valīne'mat Summoned Me to His Presence for a Talk

The next day, that is, on Sunday, we went to the guardhouse.[2] That, which is called the guardhouse, resembles a *lēylēk-chadri*.[3] But there gathered not those who planned a meeting, but noted khans gathered for entertainment. They smoked water pipes, chatted, and entertained themselves with humorous anecdotes, waiting to be summoned by the *Valīne'mat*—so that they would be ready if he called. They escorted us there and seated us.

When we gathered, dressed in our *k̲al'ats*, there were some 100 men, [maybe] more or less. The time for the *salām* arrived.

---

[1]The text has *yelpaz*.
[2]The text has *kešīk-k̲āne*.
[3]The correct term is *leyle çadir*, a night tent where the guard rests.

When we arrived to the part where we daily bowed our heads and saluted him, right then a *mīrzā* from Tabrīz, of Persian origin, from the family of J̌ahānshah, began to read. He was the *vazīr* of Azerbaijan.

It is the custom of the Persians, and the will of the *Valīnemat*, Nāder Qolī, that each city appoint three men [to supervise] the income of the royal court.

The first one is called *mīrzā-vakīl*, who together with the *ẓābet miri* is in charge of anything having to do with state income[1] and is considered the senior of the three. He orders them and is above them. He collects and disperses money and administers justice as chief *daftardar*. However, he does not act alone in his duties, but with the agreement and [participation] of the other two.

The second one is called *vazīr*. He is the middle rank. He is in charge of the provincial administration. He supervises all the income and expenses,[2] and stops criminal acts.

The third is called *mīrsofī* (*mostowfī*), who resembles the *defter-emini* (person in charge of land registry), for all the records are in his possession and he puts together the *defter* of the royal court. All the villages in various places and the *mulks* that belong to the state are under his supervision.

As I have stated, the *vazīr* of Azerbaijan, that is Atrpatakan, who belonged to the J̌ahānshah family, was also a poet and bard,[3] that is a *gusan*.[4] He, therefore, began to speak [read] that which he had created on paper. It was as follows:

Sekke'ī bezar kard nām-e salṭanat rā dar ǰahān
Ḳosrow 'ādel Šah Nāder Qolī gītī setān[5]

---

[1]The text has *ilakhay*.

[2]The text has *irat* (*irad*) and *masraf*.

[3]The text has *šuāra* from the Arabic-Persian *šā'er*, or one who excels in poetry, especially couplets or verse improvisations.

[4]A poet and troubadour.

[5]Moḥammad Kāżem has *Nāder Iran zamīn va Khosrow gītī setān*, while Moḥammad Ḥosein Qodūsī in *Nādernāmeh* (Mašhad, 1339/1960) p. 359 has:

Harkerā bāū ḳodā yārast
Harke bargardad 'ożve šarmesarast
Alḥamdolellah pādešāh-e mā nāder-e kol-e Irānast
Har bandehaš rā ḳodāy-e ta'ālā yārast
Har bandeh azū bargardad šarmesarast
Sekke'i bezar kard nāmi salṭanat rā dar ǰahān
Šah dīn Nāder Qolī Eskandar-e ṣāḥebqerān
Pādešāh-e mamālek-e Irān, ẓell-e ṣobhān, nāder-e dowrān

He announced his reign to the world by striking gold (coin)
The just monarch, the ruler of the world, Nāder Qolī.
God protects whoever follows him,
Whoever turns from him is covered with infamy.
Thank God our king is a rarity[1] in all of Iran,
God is a friend to all who serve him (are his slaves).
Those subjects (slaves) who turn from him are infamous,
He announced his reign to the world by striking gold (coin).
The king of religion, Nāder Qolī, Alexander, world ruler,
King of the Iranian lands, shadow of God, wonder[2] of our age.

Saying all this, he yelled in a loud voice, *fatiḥat*![3] All raised their hands and began to silently move their lips, as if they were saying the *fatiḥat*. I do not know if they knew it and uttered it, or not. I also stretched my hands and read, "Our Father who art in Heaven."

After the prayer was concluded, they put their hands near their face, touching their beards; while I under the influence of Christ, openly made the sign of the cross on my face.

They all moved out and left.

I stayed in my place for a short time and looked intently at the face of the *Valīne'mat*.

Šāh dīn Nāder Qolī Eskandar ṣāḥebqerān, for the second stanza which appears here in the ninth stanza.

[1]Playing on the word *nāder*—rare.

[2]Playing on the word *nāder*—wonder.

[3]The opening lines from the Qur'an.

He, therefore, looked at me and said, "O Caliph! Come here!"[1]

I gathered my courage and approached him.

He once more said, "Come closer, come closer."[2]

I approached him and stood next to where he was sitting on a high throne.[3]

He once again spoke and said, "Do you know caliph that I plan to let you leave the day after tomorrow?"[4]

I answered, "May the life and rule of my *Valīne'mat* be long. I put my hope in God, the Creator, that as I observe you today as the conqueror of Iran, I will with the help of God hope to see you as the conqueror of Qandahār and India (*Hindustān*).[5]

He laughed with happiness and gaily said, "Well done, caliph, well done!"[6]

Gathering courage after this exchange I said, "Your august one, we have one request, however, for you to fulfill."[7]

He answered immediately, "Very well. Take the caliph to Mīrzā Mumin [Mo'men] and tell him that whatever the request may be, a plan or a demand, to act upon it."[8]

Immediately a member of the *elāğājlīs*, who are constantly by his side, who are sons of khans, and who hold a decorated

---

[1]The text is in Turkish written in Armenian letters: *Hay khalifay, geal bureay.*

[2]The text is in Turkish wrtten in Armenian:*Yakhun geal, yakhun geal.*

[3]The text has *takht.*

[4]The text is in Turkish written in Armenian: *Bilirsan khalifay sabah yokh obirisi kun sani murakhas ēdēeram.*

[5]The text is in Turkish written in Armenian: *Valinamat'in omri dovlat'i ziyad olsun. Vē umaram bari khudadan parvardigēardan, ki nasêl jēnabnzi fēt'i Iran gēordum, inshallah fēt'i Ghandahar ve fēt'i Hindustanay gēorayim.*

[6]The text is in Turkish written in Armenian: *Barikallah khalifay, barikallah*

[7]The text is in Turkish written in Armenian: *Bas shefkat'lum arzamz var kearak' dur ki hasl ēdasan*

[8]The text is in Turkish written in Armenian: *Yakhshi dur dē ap'arn khalifani Mirzē Mumin yanênay vē soylan hēr nēmēnē arzasi var, mēsleht'i, mat'labi var dur ghayirsun.*

mace[1] in their hands, took me to Mīrzā Mo'men. The *mīrzā* lived near the residence of the *Valīne'mat*. He [the *elāğājlī*] passed the message of the *Valīne'mat* to him [the *mīrzā*].

The *mīrzā* responded, "I obey. It shall be done. Let his [Abraham's] *na'ib* (deputy) come this evening and take the *raqams*."[2]

Mīrzā Mo'men had been recently appointed [to his post] for preparing the *raqams*. Before that Mīrzā Mahdī wrote the *raqams*. It was Mīrzā Mahdī who also kept the seal and was the *mohrdār* (keeper of the seal). But for some reason Mīrzā Mahdī fell into disfavor. He was a wise, humble, polite, attentive, and respectable man.

The new one, that is Mīrzā Mo'men, did not yet know how to draft a *raqam* and was very timid.

But since the two *mīrzās* resided in the same house, Mīrzā Mahdī, because of the respect he had for me, prepared the necessary *raqams*.[3]

Chapter XL

On How I Received the Raqams That I Had Requested. On How the Valine'mat Called Us to His Presence and After That How He Gave Firm Instructions, Once Again Entrusting Me to the Erevan Ẓābets

The next day, I sent Vardapet Ghalayji-Oğl Step'anos, whom I had designated my traveling deputy and who was with me in the camp in Moğān [to the *mīrzā*]. He went and picked up the *raqams*, seven[4] in all, and returned happy, handing them to me.

---

[1] The text has *chomakh (čomāq)*, a club or a mace; and *nakhshats* (*naqš*), engraved, painted, or carved.

[2] The text is in Turkish written in Armenian: *Bash usdina ghayirayim. Aghsham oz nayibi gealdsun, rakhamlari ap'arsun.*

[3] Part of this paragraph is missing from MSS. *c, e, f, v1.*

[4] MS *v1* has 60.

On the same day we went to the *salām* and after the *salām* they ordered us once more, "You must come this evening and appear before the *Valīne'mat*, so that he will entrust you to your *ẓābets* and give you [final] leave to depart."

Everyone went to their quarters and stayed there until evening. In the ninth hour we gathered at the entrance to the *Valīne'mat's* residence. Myself, Kalāntar Melikjan, Melik Hakobjan, the *kalāntar* of the Armenians of Alikuli, and other *kadkodās* and Armenian meliks, for they are nine *mahals*[1]in Erevan [province] and [therefore] nine meliks--they are under the rule of the *kalāntar*, however, and tremble in his presence, like servants. The meliks are: Melik Hakobjan, Melik Mkrtum [both the meliks of the city of Erevan and its environs], and the meliks of Karbi, Kırk-Bulağ, Shuragol, Igdir, Gaṛni, Tsaghknaydzor, Gegharkun, Aparan, and Shirakovan. In addition, they took the *sheikh ul-Islam* of Erevan, as well as the *āqā* and the *mīrzās*, to the *Valīne'mat*.

He began to give instructive speeches and necessary orders concerning affairs of state, the well being of the country, the peaceful existence of *ra'yats*, and the armed troops, who were called *nokars*.[2]Since they [the *nokars*] received *donlukh*,[3]he instructed[4]the *mīrzās* regarding their [*nokars*] salaries. He said that the *nokars* had to break in their horses and had to perform their military drills. They had to take care of their horses and their equipment: armor, swords, cannon balls, daggers, shields, *terkesh* (*tarkeš*), that is a quiver with arrows, muskets, and other items were to be ready. [The equipment] given to them had to be of good quality.

He gave many other speeches in this vein concerning the security of the country and all other such maters. At the conclusion he told the *mīrzās*, "I entrust the caliph to you. If he desires anything—a village, land, or anything else which befits him more than

---

[1]*Maḥal* is a district. Nine *maḥals* are missing in MS *e*; MS *f* has it inserted by another hand.

[2]Although *nokar* (*nuker*) is translated as a servant, the *nokars* mentioned here were armed attendants or a militia.

[3]*Donluk*, which was clothing and money given to soldiers.

[4]The text has *ta'līm*.

others, give it to him in a fashion that neither the treasury suffers a loss, nor he experiences difficulties. If he does not want it then give it to others, for you know that I favor[1] him. He is a good man[2] and you have to respect him. Do not cause him to complain to me about you."

Turning to me he said, "Caliph, You are now leaving me and will not be able to talk with me. I have, therefore, entrusted you to your *ẓābets*, that is *mīrzās*. If you need anything let them know and they will fulfill your request. If they ignore your wishes, petition Ebrāhīm Khan (his brother in Tabrīz, who was a khan and *sepahsālār*)[3] and he will inform me. Pray for us. Leave, you are free, go to Üç-Kilisa."

I began to praise and thank him and with tears in my eyes I said, "Your Majesty,[4] since you are leaving us we realize that we have now become orphans. For no one will take care of us as you have done. Let the almighty God show you the way, grant you success and victory over your enemies. I also beg Your Highness: do not reduce your kindness, do not turn your sacred gaze from me and from the holy cloister [Ējmiatsin].

He once again assured me and said, " Do not grieve, caliph, do not grieve! This monastery is mine, and you are mine, go, you delightful man. Go and pray always.[5]

The *sheikh ul-Islam* then also gathered courage and read a prayer written in literary Persian, which was as long as two verses of a Psalm. After that they recited the *fatiḥat* and I recited "Father, forgive me," and then we thanked him. He gave us leave and we went to our quarters.

---

[1]The text has *khater* (*kāṭer*), "having affection for."

[2]The text has *yakhshi kishi.*

[3]Parentheses in text.

[4]The text has *shefk'et'lum* (*şevketlum*) a title used to address the Ottoman Sultan.

[5]The text is in Turkish written in Armenian script: *Alam chakmay khalifay alam chakmay. O t'ēk'ē manum dur, sanday manum san. Gēt'. Bir khoshjay kishi sen. Gēt' haman duay ēylē.*

Chapter XLI

On How We Went to See Ebrāhīm Khan and Pīr Moḥammad Khan. On the Departure of Those Who Had Come from Erevan, and How I Remained Alone

In the morning, all the men from Erevan, Armenians and Persians, began to prepare their departure. First we went to the quarters of Ebrāhīm Khan. He also assured us saying, "If you need anything, or you experience any difficulty, inform me in Tabrīz so that I may fulfill [your wishes]. For the *Valīne'mat* has given orders concerning you. Henceforth do not worry. With the help of God we shall guard the blossoming of the land."

We then went to the quarters of Pīr Moḥammad Khan, who was the khan of Erevan. He assured us even more and said, "Go in peace and freedom and do not worry about anything, for the *Valīne'mat* has entrusted you to us and has given orders regarding you. He especially loves you [Abraham] and shows concern about you. With the help of God we shall work hard to carry out all your wishes. Go in peace. The *Valīne'mat* has appointed[1] a *nā'ib* in my place to go to Erevan. He shall travel with you. Deal with him until my arrival."

We left and returned to our quarters. All those from Erevan gathered to leave—the *sheikh ul-Islam*, the notables, the *kalāntar*, the melik and *kadkodās*, together with the *na'ib* of [Pīr Moḥammad] Khan, who would function as a *muteselim* (deputy) and the *mīrzās*, all left for Erevan.

[1]The text has *ta'īn*.

Chapter XLII

On How I Remained Alone on the Plain Surrounded by a Multitude of Reed Cabins. On the Prisoners Whom I Sent to Various Places

After their departure, I remained alone, a poor, pitiful, and solitary man on the infinite plain, among a multitude of reed cabins, surrounded by my monks. "Like an owl in the ruins and like a lonely bird on the roof."[1] I redeemed [paid the ransoms for] many prisoners from their K̠orāsāni Persian slavers; some for more, others for less [money]. They gave me some of them free of charge saying, "Deliver them to their own lands and rulers." Among them were pregnant women, who had become pregnant in their own homes from their husbands, for they were in captivity for seven months. Some of them gave birth in the Moğān Steppe. I ordered the archpriest (*avagir*) of Akulis, called Vardapet T'ovmay, who was with me, to christen the babies in the river Euphrates[2] and name them Mughan. On the way to Akulis and Astabad, one woman gave birth in Meghri,[3] and they called her child Meghrik.

Among the captives there were also small girls and boys, six, eight,[4] and ten[5] years of age, as well as boys who were older, fifteen[6] to twenty years old, [maybe] older or younger. I heard that many escaped with God's help and were saved. Three times I dispatched captives on mules and camels, appointing a member from my congregation to watch over them. When the camel-drivers drove the pack animals back to Ējmiatsin, for we had no further need of them, a group of the captives went with them.

---

[1]Refers to *Psalm* 102.6-7 "I am like an owl of the wilderness, like a little owl of the waste places. I lie awake; I am like a lonely bird on the housetop."

[2]The original text has Ep'rat instead of Eraskh, an obvious error for the only rivers in the Moğān are the Kura and Arax.

[3]The main town of the Meghri region in Zangezur, Armenia.

[4]MSS. *c, d, e, v1* have seven instead of eight; MS *f* is missing "eight."

[5]MSS *c, e* are missing "ten."

[6]MS *v1* is missing "fifteen."

The rest I sent to Astabad and Akulis, for there was a shortage of bread [in the Moğān]. They took the captives on my mules to Dizak. I wrote that they be delivered to Astabad and Akulis. For Nersēs,[1] the Kat'oghikos of Aghuank' and Gandzasar[2] was there [in Dizak] and he would immediately carry out [my written instruction to him].

They loaded our mules with flour, barley, and other needed produce and returned [the mules] to us, for there was no bread and no grain in the camp. It is true that we received *t'ayin*,[3] but from the day that the *Valīne'mat* gave us leave the allotment of *t'ayin* ceased. Incidentally there was a shortage of bread not only in Moğān but everywhere: in Tabrīz, in Dizak, Ganǰe, Kazakh, Loṛi, Georgia, on the shores of Lake Sevan, in Tsaghkunadzor, in Kap'an, in Nakhichevan, and in Erevan. In the provinces mentioned one *okka* of Ottoman wheat cost one *šāhī*;[4] and even at such a price it was difficult to obtain.

When bread and flour became rare in the Moğān, we ate boiled and fried wheat, which we had brought from Holy Ējmiatsin, for a week and even longer. It is for this reason that we dispatched the freed captives to other places.

Thrice I dispatched a group of captives. The first time, I sent a party on camels and designated one of my guards,[5] Maghakia, as their leader, accompanied by two *sayis*,[6] who were from Erevan and Ējmiatsin.

The second time I sent a party of captives and designated Vardapet Sargis, the guardian of the *ambars* of Astabad, and Vardapet Eghiay from the Monastery of Hndzuts' as their leaders. They took

[1]Nerses V was the kat'oghikos of Karabagh (d. 1763). He was not a member of the Hasan-Jalaean family, the holders of the See for a considerable period. J. de Morgan, *The History of the Armenian People* (Boston, 1965), p. 413, lists him as an anti-patriarch.

[2]The monastery of Gandazar was the Holy See of Karabagh.

[3]The term is *ṭahin* (flour).

[4]A *šāhī* was equal to five silver kopeks of the time. MS *g* has "two *okka* cost two *šāhīs*."

[5]The text has shatir (*šāṭer*).

[6]Watchmen or protectors.

the captives to Dizak on our mules. I wrote to the kat'oghikos of Gandzasar, to think of a way to send them to Akulis on bullocks or donkeys. I also asked that he load our mules with provisions and return them to us accompanied by Vardapet Eghiay. Vardapet Sargis was to accompany the captives, however.

While they were on their way to Dizak, they decided to distribute *k̲al'ats* and we were ordered to go to Erevan, for it is five[1] days march from the Moğān to Dizak. I dispatched some mules to Shemakhi with Vardapet Mkrtich' of Ghap'an, who was from the T'atew monastery. He was instructed to bring food for us and our animals. For in the last few days in Moğān, wheat and barley had become more expensive. One Tabrīzi liter[2] of grain cost one *zolat'a*[3] and ten *t'imin*,[4] that is 900 *dirhams*.

On 21 February Vardapet Mkrtich' returned from Shemakhi with four mules loaded with flour, bread, barley, and wine. He was accompanied by Vardapet Israyēl from the Mesar Monastery, two priests, and five or six princes,[5] who had two requests.

First was regarding the high *ǰizya* that was demanded from them. They requested that the previous rate—three *kuruş* from a family man and one and a half *kuruş* from a single man—be reinstated.

In addition, they had concerns about their domicile, for the *Valīne'mat* had [partially] destroyed Shemakhi, when he took it prior to his arrival from Ganǰe. He constructed an earthen fortress eight[6] hours' distance from Shemakhi and ordered that the surviving citizens of Shemakhi be settled there.[7] Since the climate was unhealthy and the place was hot and had little water, and the Mus-

---

[1]MS *g* has seven.

[2]Nine livres.

[3]Brosset puts its worth at thirty *para*.

[4]Timmin was an old town in Rum, it is possible that *t'imin* was some sort of old Turkish money.

[5]MS *g* has 26 princes.

[6]MS *v1* has no "eight."

[7]Although the town was called New Shemakhi, some sources continue to refer to it as Shemakhi.

lims, that is, the Lesghians and Sunnis distressed and harassed those who suffered, that is, our people, they had repeatedly asked to be permitted to return to the old town. The Khan became so angry that he totally destroyed it.[1] Therefore, in their despair, they came to entreat me.[2]

Gathering courage, I went to the great *Valīne'mat* and asked him to order that the Armenians of Shemakhi be permitted to build a settlement near the fortress, an hour away, in a pleasant place which they themselves had selected. I asked him to give them enough land to plant orchards and plow the fields and to direct streams from the nearby river to irrigate their village and orchards. I also asked that they be permitted to build a church, for the Armenian people could not live without a church, no matter where they were, even in heaven. I also asked him about the *ǰizya* and asked that they be protected from being offended and oppressed by the non-Armenians. God's kindness softened the heart of the *Valīne'mat* and he then and there granted my requests.

He immediately presented me with the *raqams*, which were written in a mandate[3] in which the Armenians of Shemakhi were granted more than I had requested. Receiving [the *raqams*] they departed with great happiness and many thanks, blessing the Lord.

Vardapet Eghiay, who had gone to Dizak, returned on 22 February, on a Sunday. That same night they stole my horse, Ghulay, and caused me great grief, for [Ghulay] was a quiet horse and had an even pace, which suited me well.

I again redeemed captives, as many as I could; I managed to invent and to devise other ways. I borrowed money and paid for the redemption of captives. The difficulty was that the captives could not walk and there were not enough beasts of burden.

---

[1] Abraham's *Chronicle* is the only source, which states that the town was, at first, partially destroyed and abandoned and was only subsequently raised to the ground.

[2] See Commentary.

[3] The text has *buyrultu*.

Chapter XLIII

On How I Went to Dizak. On the Departure of the Ottoman Envoy, Ganǰ 'Alī Pasha. On the Departure of the Son of the Valīne'mat, Reżā Qolī Khan, to Ḵorāsān

On Monday, that is 23 February, I left the Moğān Steppe for Dizak. I crossed the bridge over the Arax and on the sixth day I arrived in a village called Tokh. Nersēs, the kat'oghikos of Gandzasar and Aghuank' awaited my arrival there.

When I departed from the Moğān I left Father T'ovmay,[1] the archpriest of Akulis, to receive more *raqams*, of which I had thought and which would be beneficial.

The *ǰulūs*[2] had not taken place yet and the *Valīne'mat* had not ascended the imperial throne. Although everything was ready, the *ǰulūs* was delayed for two reasons.

First, the seal was not carved out and the dies for the coins were not ready.

Second, his astrologers were studying [the astrological charts] and were saying that the *ǰulūs* should take place on the 25th [actually 24th] day of the moon, for that was a lucky day.

For these reasons the *ǰulūs* was delayed. But I could not remain until the day of *ǰulūs*. For one, I was weary of the long stay on the Moğān. Second, it was not proper to stay there after the *Valīne'mat* had given me leave, for that may have been interpreted as going against his command.

Thus, when the beasts of burden became available—mules and horses—I hurried to depart. When I was preparing to cross the bridge, I saw that the Ottoman envoy, Ganǰ 'Alī Pasha, was also leaving the *Valīne'mat* and departing with his retinue. He wore his *ḵal'at*, which was an overcoat[3] of heavy golden weave trimmed with expensive fur, worn the same as a *qabā*, with a hanging collar as worn by the Persians. I followed him, until we reached the en-

[1] Tuman in text.

[2] Accession to the throne.

[3] The text has *bālāpūš*.

trance of the bridge on the bank of the Arax. I halted there until the envoy and his retinue passed, for there were 300 men[1] with him.

After that I crossed as well. Following a two-hour journey, we stopped in the open, in a grassy field, for the grass was as high as it is in Rum in the month of April.[2]

The next day, that is on Tuesday 24 February, the envoy left [the Persian camp and the Moğān] for Ganǰe. After that he went through the provinces of Loṛi, Kazakh, Kars, and reached Theodovpolis.[3] ʻAbd ol-Bāqī Khan[4] the envoy[5] of the *Valīneʻmat* traveled with him. He carried gifts for Sultan Mahmud.[6] The *mehmāndār*,[7] my friend and acquaintance, Karīm Beg,[8] was also with them.

In thc same week, on Thursday, 26 February[9] (8 March N.S.),[10] on the 25th [24th] day[11] of the moon, the *ǰulūs* took place. Vardapet Tʻovmay, the archpriest of Akulis, wrote it down on paper on my order, for he witnessed it with his [own] eyes. He was in the tent of the scribes of the *raqams*, Mīrzā Mahdī and Mīrzā Moʻmen, who lived next to the residence of the *Valīneʻmat*, and saw with his [own] eyes all the ceremonies which occurred there and states that:

On that day, Thursday, at the fifth hour[12] [the *ǰulūs* took place].[13] The day before he [Nāder] sent his eldest son, Reżā Qolī Khan

---

[1] MS *v1* has 400 men.

[2] The envoy seems to have stopped as well, see next line.

[3] Thedosiopolis or Erzerum.

[4] ʻAbd ol-Bāqī Khan Zangane. MSS. e, v1 have ʻAbd ol-Qolī.

[5] The text has *ilçi*.

[6] Sultan Mahmud I (1730-1754).

[7] An officer appointed to receive and entertain a foreign dignitary.

[8] Persian sources have Mīrzā Abol-Qāsem Kāšī Ṣadr and Mulla ʻAlī Akbar Mulla-başı as accompanying the envoy.

[9] MS *v1* has 28 February. Hanway, *op cit.*, IV, 127 has 11 (22 N.S.) March, which is incorrect. Abraham's date of 8 March agrees with the Persian sources.

[10] 24 Shawwal 1148 A.H.

[11] MS *g* has 24th day of that month, which is correct. MSS. *b, d, g, v2* have 22nd day. Abraham has the 24th day of the month in the *Kondak.*

[12] MSS. *c, e, f, v1* have third hour.

[13] The text is unfinished after "the fifth hour..."

with large supplies to K̲orāsān, so that he would rule those parts as khan. He sent others to various other places. On the next day, on Thursday, he became emperor[1] in the fashion [described below].

Chapter XLIV

On How the Valīne'mat Became King and On the Ceremonies Which Took Place. On How They Seated Him [on the Throne] and Placed the Crown on [His] Head. On the Splendor Which Occurred There

When the day of the *ǰulūs* arrived, which was on Thursday 26 February,[2] on the 25th [24th] day of the moon, the khans who had remained there gathered at the fifth hour[3] at the court of the *Valīne'mat*, and placed on his head a golden crown, which resembled a helmet. Rare jewels and expensive pearls were inserted in the crown. The crown left all in a state of rapture. Mīrzā Zakī took the crown and placed it on the head of the *Valīne'mat*.[4]

They then began to pray on their knees. Only the *mukri,*[5] who was the *mulla-başı*, called Mīrzā 'Askar from Qazvīn, stood up and read the prayer. The rest of the khans who had gathered there remained on their knees with their hands raised until the end of the *du'a*, that is the prayer, which was read by the *mukri* who was standing. It [the prayer] was as long as our *voghormea*.[6] They then

---

[1]The text has *Qaiṣar* (Caesar).

[2]MS *g* has 27 February.

[3]MSS. *c, e, f, v1* have third hour.

[4]Although crowned shah, Abraham continues to refer to Nāder as the *Valīne'mat* to the end of the narrative. The reason for this is made clear only in the last section (the *kondak*), in which Abraham states that he was told that Nader had refused to accept the title of shah after the coronation. This is far from the truth. In fact, Nāder sought the title of shah and other honorific of the Ṣafavids. He would have been extremely annoyed at Abraham referring to him as *Valīne'mat* after the coronation.

[5]*Maqrī*, one who recites the Qur'an.

[6]The Armenian prayer which begins with [Lord Have] Mercy.

said the *fatihat* and prostrated themselves. They then rose and sat in their places according to rank and merit.

They began to honor those seated. First they served rose water in golden vessels; two of which were of pure gold; and one golden vessel was decorated with expensive jewels.

After the vessels with the rose water, they brought the golden censer, which in their rite is called *bukūrdān.* I have described the censer in chapter XXXIII and what they did [with it] on the first day of *bayram.* They did the same on this occasion, but even more than that time, for there were three golden and three silver censers this time.

They then served sherbet with sugar in golden cups. The vessels with the sherbet were arranged thusly: First, there was a large golden tray, which was one and a half *ḥalebi* wide. On that tray was a golden bowl filled with sherbet, which corresponded in size to that of the tray. Seeds of basil[1] floated on top of the sherbet. Another golden flagon,[2] decorated with rare and expensive jewels, caused amazement among the observers. Some said that it cost 500 *tomāns,*[3] which is 200 *kises.*[4] The flagon has been described in chapter XXXIII. In addition, there were six golden flagons and two vessels with rose water, which contained pearls, and ten[5] golden plates, on which were seven cups described in chapter XXXIII. There was the same number of golden and silver vessels.

They served [in order] first the rose water in golden vessels. They then began to spread the incense from the golden *bukūrdāns.* Then, from the golden bowl, which stood on the golden tray, they filled the golden flagon with the valuable stones; then the other golden flagons, and the silver flagons. They then filled from the golden flagon the golden cups, which stood on trays. They gave these to the khans who were seated. Those who stood were served

---

[1]The text has *reyhān.*

[2]The text has *tung* (*tange*).

[3]MSS. *c, e, f, v1* have 5,000.

[4]MSS. *b and d* have 2,000. *Kīse* or a purse of gold/silver coins.

[5]MS *e* has fifty.

in silver cups. They walked and held the censers until everyone had drunk.

Then they again prostrated themselves in front of the newly-consecrated emperor, after which they rose and each went to his own quarters.

After the departure of the khans, the middle of the tent was occupied by singers, *gusans*, young boys and girls, who sang and played musical instruments, while dancing boys danced for half an hour.

Next to the emperor was his brother, Ebrāhīm Khan, followed by his nephew, ʻAlī Qolī Beg, his [Nāder's] younger son, Mortażā Mīrzā, Mīrzā Zakī, Ṭahmāsp Vakīl Khan, and *the maʻyār başı*, that is the *ṣāheb-e ʻayār* and other intimate persons. They all stood.

After half an hour the music, singing, and dancing ceased and everyone went to his own quarters.

Two hours later, he [the king] took the golden crown off and put on his former cross-like four-cornered *Ṭahmāsī* hat, which was bound with a very thin white shawl with beautifully-embroidered two corners. The other two sides, some four fingers in length, hung on his ears. He wears it all the time.

Chapter XLV

On the Distribution of the Newly-Minted Gold Coins. On the Granting of Some New Ḵalʻats and on the Mehter-ḵāne[1]: What Does it Represent?

On the day of the *ǰulūs*, the *Valineʻmat* appointed his purveyor,[2] Āqā Zamān, as the keeper of the seal.[3]He was a Georgian who had converted [to Islam].

Mīrzā Moʻmen was appointed as the composer of *raqams* and as the head of all other scribes, or their *ra'is*.

[1]Band of musicians who played at a designated place in the palace.

[2]The text has *vakīl-e ḵarǰ*.

[3]The text has *mohrdār*.

He also comforted the former author of *raqams*, Mīrzā Mahdī, who for some reason had fallen from favor,[1] by appointing him as [official] historian and ordered him to write the history of his life and reign.

The duty of *ma'yār-başı*, that is *ṣāheb-e 'ayār*, was given to the former *ma'yār başı*, for he brought two *kīses*[2] of newly-minted coins and placed them in front of the *Valīne'mat*, who distributed them to the khans present. He also granted *ḵal'ats* to both the *mohrdār* and the *ma'yar başı*.

Then the *naqāreh*[3] *[ḵāne]* began to play, which is the Persian *mehter-ḵāne*. The *zurnas* were like the Ottoman ones, but sounded different. There was also a *ṭabl-e-bāz*,[4] which is *sādeh* (plain) *naqāreh*. There were also thirty *kiaranay*,[5] that is *boruzen*.[6] But they were not held like the Ottoman *boruzens* and their sound was not the same. They were straight and three to four *ḥalebis* long. One end, which the musician held in his mouth, was narrow, the other, as wide as a span and even more. It resembled a *boru* (horn) which is on the ships of the Latins,[7] and with which they communicate [ship to ship] at sea.

The music played and the *mehterḵāne* roared for three days without interruption, and then it stopped.

All of this as well as the *julūs* occurred after the departure of Ganj 'Alī Pasha. I departed on Monday, Ganj 'Alī Pasha on Tuesday,[8] and the eldest son of the *Valīne'mat*, Reżā Qolī Khan, left for Ḵorāsān on Wednesday. The *julūs* occurred on Thursday.

---

[1] The fall from favor is not corroborated by any Persian source.

[2] MSS. *c, e, f, v1* do not have "two kīses." The silver and gold coins were called *nāderīs* and *ašrafīs*.

[3] The *naqareh* is a drum, which is played together with a double-reed instrument, called the *zūrnā*, at official ceremonies. The *naqāreh-ḵāne* is a band of musicians in a specific location of the palace.

[4] A drum hung at the saddle.

[5] *A qarnāy*, a flute or trumpet.

[6] *A borazan* or trumpet.

[7] MSS. *c, e, f, v1* have "of the Franks" instead of "Latins."

[8] Although Abraham has departed a day earlier he met the Ottoman envoy at the bridge, see Chapter XLIII.

The autocratic and imperial deed was thus accomplished. Such is the affair and ceremony of consecration or anointment of Persian kingship according to their custom.

May God grant him [Nāder] a long and peaceful life. Let there be in his heart good will towards the country and especially to the much suffering Armenian people. Amen!

Chapter XLVI

On the Prayers Recited by the Çavuş, When the Valīne'mat Enters the Divan and When He Mounts a Horse. On the Number of His Troops

The disposition and order of the army and the type of rituals performed by the servants is as follows: When the mighty *Valīne'mat* enters the *dīvān* from the *andarūn* (inner court), thirty *çavuş* stand at the opposite side at a distance of half a stone's throw, and loudly exclaim: *In the name of Allah, the Merciful and the Compassionate. O' Allah, O'Allah! I constantly pray to thee. May your rule be firmly established. Your friend will be a friend, and your enemy shall become a friend. In honor of the greatest of Prophets, the blessing of Allah on him.*[1]

Upon mounting a horse, they exclaim: *You are the sun, the day, and the night. You are the wisest of God's creations, the most incomparable, unique, and his most marvelous handiwork.*[2]

Sometimes they exclaim: *O my lucky, gracious, beneficial, and just Khan. We constantly pray that your rule may be secure. Your friend may remain a friend and your enemy become a friend. In honor of the greatest of Prophets, the blessing of Allah on him.*[3]

---

[1]The text is in Arabic and Turkish written in Armenian characters: *Bismilahi ṛaham ṛahim. Ilahi ilahi mudami duayi mi. Dovlat'in qayim olsun. dostn dost olsun , dushmann da dost olsun. Bēhiwrmat'i siyidēlmursēlin sēlli ēlay.*

[2]The text is in Turkish written in Armenian letters: *Vē shēmsē, vē lēyli, vē nihar ēlm ul gulkilahi vahad ahgahar.*

[3]The text is in Turkish written in Armenian letters: *Fah Fah sadēt'li, shafaghat'li, inamli, adil khanêm, mudami duay mi. Dovlat'in ghayim olsun.*

Sometimes they also exclaim: *Live Long, Forever! We constantly pray, may your rule extend from one end of the world to the other. May your friend remain a friend and your enemy become a friend. In honor of the greatest of Prophets, the blessing of Allah on him.*[1]

The *çavuş* have green turbans with black bands around them. They have an ornament on their foreheads, below which there is a silver fillet the size of an apple. They carry a silver mace,[2]just like the Ottomans.

He [the ruler] also has the *hamīše kešīkčī*, that is, permanent guards [who watch him] day and night. There are 6,000 [men], every 2,000 of them guard him in turn for twenty-four hours and are then excused. After that come the next 2,000. They too guard him for a whole day and night. Then come the next 2,000. Thus the 6,000 men guard him once every three days. They are near the residence of the *Valīne'mat* at a stone throw's distance from the fence. Each ten men together with their *on-başı* occupy one hut. Five of them sleep, while the other five walk around their hut.[3] Many a time the *Valīne'mat* comes out unexpectedly and checks on them. If he finds that all, that is the ten, are asleep, he orders their execution. Therefore, they are constantly shivering, are in great terror, and fear for their lives.

He has, in addition, 300 *čandāvuls*, 300 *nasaqčīs*, and 300 *elağajlīs*.[4]There are also 1,000 more men, together with their *on-başıs*[5]and *yüz-başıs*. Their salary is as follows: *min-başıs* receive

---

Dostn dost olsun, dushmann da dost olsun. Behurmat'i sēyidēlmursēlin, sēlli ēlay.

[1]The text is in Turkish written in Armenian: *Yashay sult'anêm yashay bashdan bashay, mudami duaymi, dovlat'in bashdan bashay. Dostn dost olsun, dushmann day dost olsun, bhiwrmet'i sēyidēlmursalin selli ēlay.*

[2]The text has *chuy*, which is *čūygān*, another form for *čogān*.

[3]MS *e* has ten instead of five.

[4]MSS. *b* and *d* do not have the *čandāvuls* and the *nasaqçıs*.

[5]MSS. *c, e, f, v1* have *min-başıs*.

100 *tomāns*[1] a year; *yüz-başıs*, 36 *tomāns*; *on-başıs*, 15 *tomāns*; the troops who guard the *Valīne'mat* day and night receive 12 *tomāns*.

All the cavalrymen receive a horse from the *Valīne'mat*. If the horse dies, they bring the brand from the horse's croup and his tail as a sign [as proof for] the horse master, who is a *kāteb* (clerk) and who record the [receipt of] dead animal and the delivery of a new one. They give the horsemen a note[2] in their own hand, affixed by a seal, which enables the cavalrymen to go and receive another horse in place of the fallen one. If anyone kills a horse in one day [by riding it hard], they give him another one without any complaint. Therefore, the horsemen ride their horses mercilessly. If necessary they can travel twenty to twenty-five hours in one day.[3] There are constant strict drills for both the cavalry and infantry.

Many of the soldiers wear armor. Some had woven armor; others two metal plates, one on the chest and one on the back; others had four metal plates [on chest, back], and under their arms, one on the right and one on the left.

They also have large guns, as I have described [earlier], and large powder flasks, each one houses one and a half *okka* of powder and even more. Each one hangs two powder flasks on his back. If necessary they can gallop all day over plains and canyons, clamber and descend over rocky mountain slopes, like a partridge. They do not know tiredness, they never grumble, and sometimes they break stones to make a path between the rocks. They dig the earth and the snow, and acting as if they not labored at all, they meet the enemy bravely, give battle, and are victorious. Although I heard that he has 60,000 mercenary troops, he can if he wishes, with the help of God, in a few days gather two or three times that number.

---

[1] MS *a* has 1,000 *tomāns*; MSS. *c, e, f, v1* have 15 *tomāns*.

[2] The text has *tezkire*.

[3] MSS. *c, e, f, v1* have 15 hours.

Chapter XLVII

On How and Through What Regions I Returned to the Holy See. On How I Traveled to Visit Monasteries and to Perform Pilgrimage. On How I Investigated the Land and the Condition of the Inhabitants

When I left the Moğān on 23 February,[1] I went to the village of Tokh in Dizak, where the kat'oghikos of Aghuank', called Nersēs, a wise and well-disposed man, awaited my arrival. Although we liked each other we had never met. While on the Moğān, I, at his request, had gone to the *Valīne'mat* and had stated: "I have appointed a deputy and have given him the title of Caliph of Ganǰe, and the House of Gandzasar, land of the Aghuank', Shemakhi, and Shirvan, so that he may rule over the monasteries, churches, and the [Armenian] population. For the region is far away from my domain and I am not able [to manage it]. But sheep cannot live without a shepherd. The khans of Ganǰe and the *ẓābets* sow discord and by their action disturb the peace, constantly robbing and pillaging. Therefore, I beg Your Highness, that from now on neither should the khans nor the sultans, nor the *ẓābets*, makes any demands from him. He is my *vakīl* and *nā'ib*. If they have any demands let them come to me." He gave me a [suitable] *raqam* and I handed it to Kat'oghikos Nersēs. He was extremely happy and together we celebrated the pre-Lent feast[2] in Tokh and Hadrut.[3] On Monday, at the start of Lent,[4] I departed from Hadrut.

Although some of the meliks of Khachen,[5] Varanda,[6] and Avetaranots'[7] came to see me with gifts and presents, and asked me to

---

[1]MSS. *b* and *v2* also have the fifth day of the week; MS. *d* has Thursday; MS *g* has 24 February.

[2]The text has *parekentakan*.

[3]The main town of the Hadrut region in Mountainous Karabagh.

[4]Since Easter was on 25 April, Lent must have started on 8 March.

[5]One of the five main districts of Mountainous Karabagh, see map.

[6]One of the five main districts of Mountainous Karabagh, see map.

[7]Another name for Chanakhchi, the main town of Varanda.

visit their districts, I refused. For there was a great shortage of wheat and barley and there were many men and beasts with me. Secondly, I wanted to hurry home and rest. My body was in a hurry, for I was weary of wandering and of the cold, especially since my nose and one of my ears was stuffed up. I was tired and agitated.

I, therefore, hurried and arrived in the village of Dzorkegh and from there to the village of Bnadzor, and from there to the nomad camp of Ghoṛch'ibēk, who was from P'isian, and from there to Khndzorek,[1] which is located between large rocky mountains and has an immeasurable height. We descended through a narrow path into the gorge and saw an amazing sight. Fearing the Ottomans and the Karaçorli Kurds, the [Armenian] peasants had abandoned the village, which was located in the valley. They had carved in the hardest rocks on both sides of the gorge caverns, which they called *magharay*.[2] Each person had hollowed out a living quarter for his family and they lived there. The amazing thing was that they ascended and descended these [gorges with the aid of] leather straps. The women would tie their infants to their backs, and they would also tie a jug of water and other necessary items and also with the help of the belt climbed and entered the high rocky gorges. Then they pulled the rope of belts up and thus no stranger could enter [their homes]. Their homes [in the village] were destroyed by Ottoman troops and robbers—bandits from the Karačorli Kurds.

Previously there were 500 households[3] in Khndzoresk, but there are fewer today, for many were killed by the Turks. The reason was that the Turks and their army had repeatedly attacked the Armenians and were shamefully beaten back [in other bastions]. They had succeeded, however, in taking one side of the ravine [of Khndzoresk], where the inhabitants did not have caverns, to aid each other. The Turks had taken the women and children as booty, had slaughtered the men with swords, and had left. Thus only some half or one-third of the inhabitants had survived. Those who were

---

[1]Khndzoresk is a village in the Goris district of Armenia.

[2]The correct term is the Arabic/Persian *maġā'er*.

[3]MSS. *c, e, f, v1* have 300.

saved had caverns facing each other and managed, with the help of guns, to defend each other from the enemy.[1]

Previously they wove superb carpets and small rugs,[2] but there are fewer weavers today and it is very difficult to find old weaver women.

These peasants escorted us through deep snow. They were armed and had guns. They brought us to the great monastery of T'atew. On the way there was a devastated village which they called Karahunj.[3] The inhabitants of this village were excommunicated by the head of the T'atew monastery.[4] They begged me to lift the anathema from them. I conceded and gave them absolution and blessed the village, where there was a magnificent church, built from smoothly polished stones.

I remained four days in the monastery. While we were in the monastery, on Tuesday, 16 March, at the seventh hour[5] of the evening of the fast the weather had cleared. The moon was full, for during my journey to the monastery snow had fallen for 24 hours. It had cleared. Without telling anyone, I secretly left my cell and went to the entrance of the monastery and saw that half of the moon was dark. By the time it had risen completely it had become totally dark and hidden.[6]

---

[1] These were the so-called *sghnag* (*sığınak*) or mountain shelters, described in the *History of Dawit' Beg*, in Brosset's, *op. cit*, II, 229.

[2] The text has *khali* (*qālī*) and *qālīče*.

[3] A village in the Goris district of Armenia.

[4] There is no explanation as to the reason for this action.

[5] MS *v1* has fifth.

[6] The full eclipse of the moon occurred on 26 March 1736 at midnight.

Chapter XLVIII

On How I Went On a Pilgrimage, First to the Great Monastery of Haṛants',[1] Which is Located Below the Monastery of T'anahat

On the day after the eclipse of the moon, I took some of the vardapets and members of the congregation with me, and traveled on a pilgrimage to the formerly great monastery of Haṛants', which was considered the mother of all the Armenian monasteries in the East and West. In the chapel where the blessed remains of the saintly vardapets, Pōghos and Sargis, and the monks Aristakēs and Barsegh, are buried, about whom the chronicler Aṛakel writes in chapter XXV.[2] Our pilgrimage completed, we examined the monastery and the high mountain, where they [the saints] had died. The mountain had split, the earth had shaken,[3] and the cemetery was thrown open and had moved a distance of an arrow's flight and had come to a stop. The chapel, where the remains of the aforementioned saints were had also [been damaged]. After our pilgrimage we conducted the noon service[4] at the monastery. We then went down to the chapel, which was a small church, where the graves of the aforementioned saints were located, and performed an evening service there.

We crossed the Vorotan River, which flows between the chapel and wooden monastery of Shēnhēr,[5] on horseback and went up to the monastery and I saw that it was in ruins and devoid of people. In the past some 150 monks had resided there, but now only twenty[6] lived there and these were perturbed and desperate. We

---

[1]Northwest the T'atew monastery, in Zangezur region of Armenia. According to Alishan it was constructed in the 17th century. It is currently in ruins.

[2]Refers to the History of Aṛakel of Tabrīz, but the section is in chapter XXII not XXV, see p. 218 of Khanlaryan's translation, Moscow, 1973 (critical text). MSS. *b, d, v2* have chapter 22.

[3]A major earthquake had occurred there on 25 April 1658.

[4]The text has *zham* (divine service, canonical hours).

[5]Northeast of the T'atew monastery, near the village of Shinuayr in the Goris region of Armenia.

[6]The text has two tens, Brosset (II, 316) has read this as two and ten (12).

performed a night service there and since it was already nightfall, we spent the night there.

At dawn, following the morning service, I comforted the monks and [promised to give them] whatever they church utensils they lacked: drapes, iron [bars] for the drapes, books, attires for each of them, a chalice, and a cross. The gallery on the top, where men visiting the monastery stand, was in ruins. Therefore, I immediately ordered them to find a carpenter, timber and boards. I paid the master and [for] the materials, and I ordered that the work be completed right away.

I then departed and passing through the village of Haludzor[1] I once again reached the T'atew Monastery. On 18 March I went up to thc upper monastery and stayed seven days there, until the snow was reduced and the road became passable. I also sent to the women's cloister church utensils, which I managed to obtain in the T'atew village. Since there was no bread, I ordered that the monastery give the miserable [women] some seeds.

I then left the monastery and traveling through the depopulated village of Tandzavēr, we reached the village of Irits'vanik. From there, through Bargushat, to the village of Giwlmēshē, which belonged to Melik Shrvēn. After that, we came to a small town called Amarat'.

Paron Hovhann, the *shahvek'il* (district supervisor) came out to greet us there. We took him with us and went on through a difficult road until we reached the village of Malev,[2] after which Paron Hovhann took us to his village of Kaler. Two days later we returned to Malev by the same road. After performing the noon mass and resting a short while we reached the village of Kaṛaw.

After that we reached Meghri, where there was a small, respectable and delightful monastery. I spent three days there comforting them as well. Traveling through the village of Karchevan,[3] we ar-

[1]Halidzor is a village in the Goris district of Armenia.

[2]Malev or Manlev is a village in the district of Arevik (Meghri), where Armenians under the leadership of Prince Toros, had, a decade earlier, fought the Muslims during the era of national awakening led by Dawit' Beg.

[3]A Village in the Meghri region of Armenia.

rived to Ordubad, and from there on 6 April we reached the big village of Dasht.

On 7 April, the Feast of the Annunciation, we were invited to lead the Divine Liturgy. Obliging their request, we performed the Holy Sacrament.

The next day the princes of Goght‘ arrived, accompanied by their religious hierarchy and invited us to Akulis. I remained there until Holy Easter and New Sunday,[1] for the monastery of St. Thomas the Apostle is enchanting and amazes all who see it. My spiritual son, Prior Hovhannēs, the well-behaved, mild-mannered, and brilliant vardapet, was an old acquaintance of mine. It was out of my love for him and because of my pilgrimage to the monastery, which occurred on the first Sunday, as well as the supplication of the inhabitants, that I remained there so many days. They invited me to the four churches located there to lead services there and to bless them on Sundays and other appropriate days. That is precisely what happened.

On that same day, on Red Sunday,[2] after performing the holy liturgy, I installed as bishop, the archpriest of Akulis, Father T‘ovmay, a member of the congregation of Holy Ējmiastin.

On Monday after the first Sunday, I departed from there and arrived in Ts‘ghnay, at the monastery of Miwzkiwnay. From there [I proceeded] to Old Julfa, and from Julfa to Darashamb. Crossing the Arax by boat at the junction where the river Tghmut empties into the Arax, I went up to the marvelous monastery of St. Step‘annos, the first martyr. This was on 7 May and I stayed in that monastery for nine days.

I then went to the Church of St. Karapet in Erinjak, for I had visited it previously, on my way to the Moğān. Two days later I went to Gagh and after that to Shorot‘,[3] to visit the Shorot‘ monastery and hermitage.

[1] The Octave of Easter.

[2] Third Sunday after Easter.

[3] A small village in Goght‘, it had been a trade center, presently in Nakhichevan.

The son of the late Paron Aqamal, my old friend, Paron Aghek'sandr, invited me to his house. In the evening we once again went up to the church of St. Illuminator.

At dawn we traveled to P'aṛaka[1]and alighted at the monastery. From there we traveled to the village of Tiwi, where there stood the abandoned and uninhabited monastery, while the nunnery had only seven in seclusion. After visiting them, I left the same day and arrived in the large village of Bust, where there was an excellent church.

After visiting the church, I climbed up to the monastery, which resembled a dove and was like heaven. It was [situated] in a beautiful and lofty place, with many irrigated gardens and fertile earth, with clean and life-giving air. My heart was filled with happiness and I forgot the difficulties of the journey. Their superior, Vardapet Petros, a wise and gentle priest, as well as the monks and brothers received me with love and humility. I stayed two days here.

I departed from there and after passing a number of villages, I arrived at the large village of Kazanchi. I stayed three days there and because of their requests and supplications, I led the noon service there. Traveling through that village I reached Norashenik, and from there, once again to the church of St. Karapet in Erinjak, from where I traveled to Nakhichevan and stayed two days there. After that I stopped at the blessed city of Astabad, in a beautiful and wonderful Astabad monastery.

There are many monasteries in our land—one more magnificent than the other, one more beautiful than the other, bringing admiration to those who see them.

Alas! These are troubled times, my downtrodden people. My heart is pressed when I see splendid monasteries and holy cloisters, for there are not enough congregations and priests. Although there are monasteries, they are empty, uninhabited, and devoid of people. There are some impoverished villages, but they are in no condition to help the monasteries, satisfy their needs, or fulfill their

---

[1]A village previously populated by Armenians, presently in the Nakhichevan region.

requirements. They are in need of help themselves from the monasteries.

On Sunday, the day of the Apparition of the Holy Cross,[1] I performed the Holy Sacrament in Astabad and appointed three bishops: the first of them was Vardapet Gēorg from Isfahan, at the request of the prelate Vardapet Astuatsatur and the local princes. The second, I appointed as the bishop of the monastery of St. Bartholomew the Apostle, which was located in Urumiye, at the request of the inhabitants of that diocese. The third was Vardapet Melkon of Kaffa, a member of the Ējmiatsin brotherhood.

I then left Astabad and safely arrived in Holy Ējmiatsin on 12 June. This was an occasion of great joy for all the members of the congregation and the entire Ararat province. Giving thanks to God Almighty, our Protector, the Creator of and the Deliverer from possible misfortunes, I prostrated myself in front of the place of the Holy Descent in the great and universal cathedral, with its great wailing and mournful walls. I once again entrusted myself to God with the prayers of our Holy Father, Gregory the Illuminator.

Chapter XLIX[2]

On how the Ẓābets, Yüz-başıs, Āqās, Kalāntars, and Meliks of the Ararat Province Departed for Tabrīz to Congratulate Ebrāhīm Khan on His Arrival and His Elevation to the Rank of Sepahsālār, and to Submit the Accounts of the State Treasury

Ebrāhīm Khan arrived in Tabrīz, with the title of *Sepahsālār*, for he was the second [in command] after the king, being the brother of the King/*Valīne'mat*, and took possession of his seat and settled in.

He then invited the *ẓābets* of the Erevan district dīvān. He also invited the *āqās*, the *kalāntars*, the *meliks*, and the *kadḵodās*, who

[1] The text has *mets`ahrash*, the fourth Sunday after Easter.
[2] The text has forty-ninth.

gathered for the journey, prepared gifts, and hurried to depart for Tabrīz.

I was also invited. But since I was ill and tired from my journey, I did not go, but dispatched the vardapet of Akulis, T'ovmay, with appropriate gifts and with requests. I asked Ebrāhīm Khan to give me the necessary *raqams* regarding monasteries, and building and restoring churches and the land.

He immediately gave the *raqams* and fulfilled all my requests, granting me two more *raqams* than I had requested.

The first made the position of the kat`oghikosate exalted and eminent, which preserved its authority.[1]In the second, he entrusted me to the khan of Erevan or [in his absence] to his deputy.

He also sent me a *k̲al'at*, which consisted of a chasuble. Since fine cloth was not found at the time among the merchants, he ordered that two of his own *qabās*, sewn from a fine material, be undone, and a chasuble prepared. He sent it [the chasuble] to me.

He also gave a *k̲al'at* to Vardapet T'ovmay, whom I had sent to him, robing him in a golden-weave *qabā* and a magnificent girdle. He also robed [*k̲al'at*] the *mīrzā*, who was like a *baş-defterdār*, as well as the *kalāntars*, meliks, and other notables who had traveled to Tabrīz. After he had robed them he was pleased and granted them leave. Soon, after a few days, they arrived with great happiness and triumph, to Erevan.

Chapter L[2]

On How Ebrāhīm Khan, on the Order of the King, His Brother, Invited Me to Tabrīz, Accompanied by the Mīrzā and the Kalāntars and Others

In September, when I was in Hovhannavank' and was busy with the reconstruction of the Church of St. Karapet, there came an in-

---

[1]The text has *serefrazutean, which is ipka*, from the Persian *sar-āfrāz* and the Arabic *'ibqā'*.

[2]The text has fiftieth.

vitation and an order from Ebrāhīm Khan. One of his main and loyal *čāpārs* (courier) carrying the order came to Erevan and had it read [aloud] for those who were to depart.

He also sent me an invitation, which was written separately to me. I was very ill, following my agonizing fever, and was on the construction site in Hovhannavank'. I read the note, learned of its content, and went to Erevan so that I would learn the reason [for the invitation].

But they were also astounded, especially Mīrzā Kāżem, who was terribly afraid that someone had sent a complaint against him to Ebrāhīm Khan.

He began to appeal to me with a request for protection and through Vardapet Aghek'sandr sent a message promising Holy Ējmiatsin and me numerous rewards, provided I save him, if Ebrāhīm Khan was angry with him and had decided to kill him.

In addition, he asked about the *čāpār*. He asked me to take him [*čāpār*] to Ējmiatsin and keep him there, until he [Mīrzā Kāżem] compiled the register of all the state income from the Ararat province. I took the *čāpār* with me and returned to Ējmiatsin, for Ebrāhīm Khan had given the *čāpār* orders stating: "Do not dare to offend or distress the caliph, for he is an old man. Let him do as he wishes."

After a few days, however, he [the *čāpār*] returned to Erevan, so that he would force them to depart. I again implored the *čāpār*, as he was preparing to leave for Erevan, to wait a little longer. After five or six days, I having been sick, got up and went to Erevan and told the *čāpār* and the *mīrzā*, "I shall slowly go to Astabad and will wait for you there." I began my journey. The *kalāntars*, both the Armenian ones and those belonging to the outsiders (Muslims), traveled with me. Thus, moving slowly, we reached Astabad. After three days' stay we moved on, together with the princes from Nakhichevan, Paron Astuatsatur and Paron Kharisimos. We traveled on the Tabrīz road.

When we reached the little town of Marand, situated near Tabrīz, some twelve hours of travel away, they, that is, the *mīrzā*, the *čāpār*, and the *yüz-başı* caught up with us. After resting in Marand for a day, we arrived in Sofiyān[1] and went from there to Tabrīz.

The next day we went and sought an audience with the *sepahsālār*, bearing gifts, each one according to his status. He received us with great affection and very, very gently reassured us.

He especially called me to his presence and told me many comforting and encouraging words.

When he observed that due to the long fever my face was as pale as a dead person's he became angry at the *čāpār* saying: "Why did you bring the caliph? He is sick!" I answered, "My Khan, even if I was on my death bed, I would want them to bring me to you in my coffin, for when I look at you, I see in you and in your face, the *Valīne'mat*, which shall comfort me before I die."

He again reassured me and was very pleased. He ordered that the *kalāntar*, and the Armenian princes, and I, be housed together in one place. Among them was Paron Step'an from Akulis, for the princes had arrived in Tabrīz a few days earlier, to find out the contents of the decree issued by the *Valīne'mat*.

We went and settled in one of the houses inside the fence [of his residence]. They read the *raqam* in our presence and discussed it, within our hearing range. Hearing it we were very happy, for the decree was composed of two parts: the first was on entrusting the region to Ebrāhīm Khan. The second was about me in particular. It was addressed to Ebrāhīm Khan ordering him to deal graciously with me and to always treat me gently, to listen to what I had to say and to fulfill my requests. (Thank God, the Almighty! My thoughts are full of rapture! Why and for what reason does He place so much affection, thoughtfulness, and care in the heart of this mighty man and autocrat? Praise Thee God! Your love of man is ineffable!).[2]

When we learned about the decree of the king, his brother, they took us again to him [Ebrāhīm Khan]. After he chatted with us for a long time, he once more called me to his presence and uttered

---

[1]A small town in the municipality of Tabrīz in Iranian Azerbaijan.

[2]The parentheses are in the original text.

many speeches and told funny jokes and laughed with me and his *mīrzā*, who was called Mīrzā Rāẓī.

Chapter LI[1]

On the Story of Mīrzā Rāẓī, Who was the Vakīl and Ẓābet of the Province of Nakhichevan. On the Girl from Astabad, Whose Nokar Had Forcibly Abducted, Converted, Married[2] and Had Brought Her to the Moğān. On How I Took Her Back with the Help of God, Returned Her to the Armenian Faith, and Married Her to a Christian Youth

When I was traveling to the Moğān, this *mīrzā* was the *ẓābet* and ruler of Nakhichevan. He was very arrogant, inhumane and hated Christians.

After our departure, one of his servants, called Dawit‘ (Dāvūd), kidnapped the daughter of a Christian, forced her to renounce her Christian faith and to marry him. He had brought her to the Moğān Steppe. The father of the girl followed him, crying, accompanied by a *maḥẓar* (petition) from Astabad, came to the Moğān. I, therefore, made a complaint against the *mīrzā*.

We argued for a long time in front of the *Valīne‘mat*. I even told the *mīrzā*, "You have ruined the region of Nakhichevan, have left no property for the *ra‘yats*, [the situation has become so bad] that your *nokars* openly struck the melik of Astabad with an axe and killed him. They took the daughter of a Christian from her house in the night [armed] with swords, forcibly converted her and made her marry. You have now swallowed over 1,000 *tomāns* of bribes from the Nakhichevan region. And if the king orders I shall demand an accounting, for the money of the *ra‘yats* belongs either to them or to the king. Why did you devour it?"

The very wise *Valīne‘mat* immediately ordered that they throw him to the ground, face down. Six men began to beat him, from his

[1]The text goes back to fifty-one instead of fifty-first.
[2]The text has the term *kābīn*.

neck to the tendons of his feet. After [they gave him] many blows, he cried out, "I have something to say!"

They raised him to his feet and brought him [to the *Valīne'mat*]. He ordered [him] to speak. We also began to speak, for with me were present the princes of Nakhichevan, Parons Astuatsatur, Kharisimos, and Step'annos of Akulis.

They tied him once more [and threw him to the ground] face down and beat him so hard, that he lost consciousness twice or thrice. When he came to he screamed again, "I have something to say!" Once more, on the order of the great one, they brought the *mīrza* to him. He ordered [him] to speak. [The *Valīne'mat*] himself found that [his words] were false, for we did not speak anymore.

The *Valīne'mat* ordered that they administer the *falake*.[1] They raised [his feet] and began to strike his soles, until finally he fainted.

Witnessing the torture which that man was experiencing, I was sorry that I had filed the complaint. I began to beg the *Valīne'mat*, not in words, but by meekly raising my hands, shedding tears with a broken heart and bent head. I continued in this fashion until the [*Valīne'mat*] noticed and realized that I desired to beg him to cease torturing that man, but was afraid to do so. He immediately ordered the strikers to pull back and to lift him on his feet and bring [the *mīrzā*] to him. Two men, grabbed him by his underarms and dragging him put him in front of the *Valīne'mat* and with difficulty [forced him] to stand. [The *Valīne'mat*] ordered him to compose an account of the management of the land tenure and to make a list of what he had taken [for himself] and to hand it to him [*Valīne'mat*]. He [the *mīrzā*] fainted once more in front of the *Valīne'mat* and they dragged him out. They assigned one of the *elāğājlī* [to act] as a *mobāšer*.

The *Valīne'mat* once again comforted and reassured us, saying "Take the abducted girl and give her to the caliph." They fulfilled his order immediately and took the girl from her husband. I treated the kidnapper of the girl severely and said, "I want you to give a

[1]Bastinado.

divorce decree and seal it in front of witnesses, stating in writing that from this moment the girl is released from you and that you will not have any litigation over her with her parents. Although he tried to get rid of me by thinking up various excuses, for he was in love with the girl, he did not rid himself [of me]. They ordered him to immediately write that which I had demanded and to get a new seal, for he did not have a seal with him. He gave me [the decree] affixed with a seal and signed by many witnesses; only then was he rid of me.

The amazing thing was that during the time when that filthy man [the kidnapper] was especially flushed, suffered and cried, there came a number of notables; among them [were] even khans, and with delicacy and flattery begged me to give the girl to him and not to separate them from each other, "for—said they—you are committing a great sin." They continued to implore [me]. Then, as a last resort, I said, "In that case give me a Muslim girl in her place, so that I would marry her to a Christian youth. I shall then give her to you." After that they gave up hope and moved away from me.

I once again demanded that they give me a decree regarding the girl [stating] that she was to remain in her faith and was to marry a Christian, and that the abductor was not permitted to bring a law suit, and that the *ẓābets* of the region should not involve themselves in matters of faith. For she had renounced the Christian faith in the presence of the *sheikh ul-Islam* and the *qāẓī* of Nakhichevan. They granted me the *raqam* according to my wishes. Handing the daughter and the *raqam* to the father, I rushed them to Astabad, so that on arrival the father would marry her to someone. They did so immediately and the father gave her to some young man. They now live, glorifying God the miracle maker.

Following that I sat with the *mīrzā*, after they had wrapped him in a warm sheepskin to reduce his pain. Recovering he sat with us to give an account.

There were 82 villages in the Nakhichevan province. Seven hundred *tomāns* in bribes had been taken from 32 villages, which he had pocketed. After long supplications we forgave him 200 *tomāns*. The [remaining] 500 *tomāns*,[1] which makes 20 *kises*, were presented to the *Valīne'mat,* who was informed of the proceedings. But the *Valīne'mat* did not agree and right then ordered the *mobāšer* that the *mīrzā* had three days to gather the rest of the sum. He did and gave [the money] and was relieved from the wrath of the *Valīne'mat*.

He was also deprived of the title of *mīrzā* and *ẓābet* of Nakhichevan, fell from favor and was banished. But since the *mīrzā*'s father had for a long time, long before this [event] performed services for the *Valīne'mat*, the *Valīne'mat's* brother, Ebrāhīm Khan, appointed him as his *mīrzā* and kept him in his service. [Mīrzā Rāẓī] is now with Ebrāhīm Khan in Tabrīz. Everything that takes place in the court of the khan is done with his participation; without him nothing happens.

Since the khan knew all about this affair, he began to laugh and joke with me. And since I had become sallow and pale because of my illness, he thought that [I had changed color] due to suspicion or embarrassment. He therefore said repeatedly, "Caliph, you are my father and I am your son, I swear by everything and anything. Indeed if in your heart you have misgivings and doubts regarding Mīrzā Rāẓī, I shall expose him to the same tortures, or if you wish I shall kill him."

I replied with a groan, "Not [necessary] my khan, for both he and his father are loyal servants of your clan. And if something happened in the Moğān, the cause of it was his servants, for they were terribly undisciplined and he had not restrained them. We serve you for two reasons: first, for our faith, so that we can freely profess our Christian faith; second, to guard the chastity of our families. Therefore, this [*mīrzā*] is aware that if we had continued our litigation until its conclusion, he would not have escaped death. For on that day when they were torturing him, I twice begged with signals and he was saved. Otherwise he was threatened by death.

---

[1]MSS. *b* and *g* have 700 *tomāns*.

We have now made peace. Under your rule, during your lifetime, after God, I do not fear any man, for it does not do for me to serve you and fear others. Others have to fear me!"

He was very pleased and with great affection gave us leave to return to our quarters.

Chapter LII

On How Ebrāhīm Khan Feted Us at His Table Day and Night and on the Next Day Presented Me with an Expensive Ḵal'at

Two days later, he [Ebrāhim Khan] once again invited us to a celebration in our honor. For it is customary for the Persians to invite a person whom they wish to honor, at midday, what they called *ch'ashd*,[1] for lunch and for dinner in the [same] day. He thus honored us with a celebration at lunch and dinner, sat with us and made us happy. At dinner we were joined by Mīrzā Kāżem of Erevan, Kalāntar Melikjan, and the notables of Nakhichevan, that is Parons Astuatsatur, Kharisimos, and Step'an. At two o'clock at night Ebrāhīm Khan let us go and we went back to our residence filled with great joy.

The next day he again invited and presented [us] with *ḵal'ats*. I received a golden-woven mantle with an astonishing hem. A number of people assured me that only the shah or the *vālī* could wear a *ḵal'at* of such quality. The *mīrzā*, the *kalāntar*, and the three notables [received] a *qabā* of golden weave, a girdle, and a fur cloak each. We were dressed in the *ḵal'ats* at the house of the *mīrzā* [Rāẓī] and we then went to Ebrāhīm Khan for the *salām*. He once again spoke at length with us, giving instructions and assurances. He again affectionately joked with me in a manner that I cannot express in writing. I then said, "My khan, you have to give me a number of necessary *raqams*, like your kin [brother] the *Valīne'mat*." He immediately told the *mīrzā*, "Quick, swiftly fulfill

[1]Probably *jašn*, a banquet which lasted from noon to midnight, or *čašīdan*, to taste various delicacies.

all that the caliph asks, according to his wishes, so that they can leave."

The *mīrzā* invited me to his quarters to honor me. We did as he wished and went to his residence for lunch and dinner. We talked and discussed the events that had occurred on the Moğān. He began to beg and apologize, stating: " It was my fault that I did not get to know you and it was especially the fault of my servant for causing my calamity." Next to him sat his 15-year[1]old son, who had just arrived from K̲orāsān. The *mīrzā* put his hand on the head of his only son and took the firm oath, saying "In my heart and in my mind I do not have any hatred or envy toward you. I beg you to forget about the past and to entreat Ebrāhīm Khan as well as write to the *Valīne'mat* displaying good heartedness and plead for us." We thus broke bread and reconciled, leaving the rest in God's hand, for it is said in the [Proverbs] of Solomon, "when an enemy speaks graciously, do not believe it, for there are seven abominations concealed within."[2]

After that I asked him to write thirteen *raqams*,[3]some of them in the form of the *raqams* given to me by the *Valīne'mat*. Others were new requests concerning monasteries, churchmen, the land, and the peasants.

After we had spent sixteen days in Tabrīz, [Ebrāhīm Khan] gave us leave. Those who had come with me left swiftly, but I stayed another three or four days in Tabrīz and then I departed as well.

---

[1]MS *g* has 20-year old.
[2]*Proverbs*, 26.25.
[3]MSS. *a* and *g* have 15 *raqams*.

Chapter LIII

On How I Returned from Tabrīz to the Holy See. On How the Vakīl of Nakhichevan, Who was the Nā'ib, Honored Us as His Guests

When I left Tabrīz and reached the bank of the Arax, at the crossing point, the *nā'ib* of Nakhichevan, Āqā Hasan of Korāsān, a well-mannered, wise, humble, and mild man, sent a message [in which he displayed] his affection for me. He had a man waiting for me at the river crossing, inviting me to Nakhichevan as his guest.

In reply, I said that I am an old man, ill and shall go to the Astabad monastery to rest there a few days and after that on my way to Erevan, I shall stop at Nakhichevan and stay one night as his guest, before I continued on. That is what happened, for I first went to Old Julfa and spent a night there.

In the morning I went to Astabad monastery and spent 12 days in the monastery.

Then, together with Paron Astuatsatur, we went to Nakhichevan, which was near Astabad, a half an hour's ride. This occurred on Saturday, 20 November. The *na'ib* of Nakhichevan, Āqā Ḥasan, who had invited us to be his guests, rode out to greet us. With him were also other *mīrzās* and the khan of Nakhichevan, Valī-Qolī, the *yüz-başı*, and other notables, more than two hundred[1] horsemen. They led us into the city of Nakhichevan.

When we reached the center of the town, a place resembling a theater, surrounded on all four sides by shops, there were numerous idle onlookers. The khan invited us to his court to honor us, but Āqā Ḥasan did not permit it. They got off their horses and argued for a long time. The khan pulled me to his side and the *mīrzā* to his.

The moment I realized that this will lead to an argument and that they were preparing to throw abuses each other--for one of them was a khan and the other, the *vakīl* of the king, having the duty of the king's notary and placed in charge of collecting reve-

[1] MS *f* has 20.

nues—I swiftly got off my horse and stood between them. I implored them and kissed their beards and barely stopped the fight. I made an agreement with Āqā Ḥasan, saying, "You are brothers, therefore it is not proper for you to insult each other on my account. I am your guest, let it be as he wishes, we shall go to his house, have lunch, and then we will go to the house of Your Excellency and if you wish I shall spend a whole month with you."

I thus succeeded in making peace between them. We first went there where the khan had invited us. Then we went to the house of the *nā'ib*. We stayed there until Tuesday. Our party consisted of thirty vardapets and *nokars* and thirty-two horses and mules.

On Tuesday we embarked with great ceremony with the standard of the cross before us and peacefully traveled through Sharur and Artashat to the Virap monastery. From there to Noragavit and on Saturday, 27 October, we reached the Holy See of Ējmiatsin.

The entire congregation and the peasants came to greet us with great solemnity. There were many Ottomans in the village [Vagharshapat] and observing the light of our faith and the solemnity of our ceremonies they were delighted, surprised, and astounded. Entering beneath the dome of the great and universal holy cathedral's life sustaining world, I prostrated myself before the place of the Holy Descent uttering innumerable blessing and glory to God, bowing [before Him]. Covered with tears of happiness we informed all the members of the congregation, as well as those who had gathered there—the church was full of our people and Muslims—of the reason we had been summoned, about our journey, on how they had honored us, and how [Ebrāhīm Khan] had robed us in *k̲al'at*. Those who heard [our narrative] were surprised and full of wonder and gave glory to God. After that I performed a prayer, blessed all who were present, and we let everyone go in peace.

Āqā Ḥasan, who had invited me to his house, gave me an expensive chasuble, that is a *k̲al'at* from silk, embroidered with golden thread.

May he be blessed and rewarded by God for that. I truly wonder at this man's gentleness and humility. His affection for me was no pretence but true, for with the help of God we have learned to identify hypocrites, who abound. But this man is devout and I dare say, in the depth of his soul, worships God, a believer. He has entranced and enraptured me and everyone else, with his gentleness and humility, May God reward his belief and labors, and all other friends and good deed doers of the Holy See.

First, the *Valīne'mat* and his brother, Ebrāhīm Khan, and all the khans, governors of regions and provinces, sultans, and *mīrzās*, and notables, in general all those who show concern for me, for the congregation, its members, my people, and especially for the Holy See, who love us, show concern for us, and display kindness toward us: may God grant them a long life, success and reward for their goodness in this and the next world. Amen!

This is the end of my narrative. I ask that the readers of this effort of love not blame me for its verbosity and its simplicity, for I have tried, according to my ability, to make the narrative short, clear, and understandable to all. For, if I had recorded in order all that happened there would have been not enough paper or ink. I have written enough that those who wish to learn about the events and conditions in the Holy See and about my [situation] could find the answers in this true account and be satisfied. If the account meets your expectations then it is God's kindness. If not, forgive me for my slow pace, for I wrote it while suffering and in the midst of much work, afflicted, tortured and strained, being ill and weak. Stay well![1]

[1]The text has *voghj leruk'*.

The Kondak[1] of Kat'oghikos Abraham of Crete[2]

The servant of Jesus Christ, Reverend Abraham, Kat'oghikos of All Armenians and Patriarch of Vagharshapat [which is] full of light and populated by angels and throngs of seraphims and gatherings of cherubs, the all-embracing, heaven-like, the illustrious, the pure, the divine, the great, the unconquerable See of Vagharshapat, Holy Ējmiatsin, from where with tender affection and permanent yearning, desires, and with greetings, endowed with God's abundance to the Holy See of [where Jesus Descended] Christ, I address you, my beloved ones, part of my soul, *mahtesi*[3] Harut'iwn, *mahtesi* Seghbos, *mahtesi* Astuatsatur, *mahtesi* Baghdasar, and to all the others who are with you, I wish you eternal happiness in the glory of God and in [the glory] our Holy Church.

Let it be known to you, my beloved ones who are dear to my heart, that in September and November I twice or thrice, or maybe even more, wrote briefly and informed my son, the Patriarch of Constantin[ople],[4] of past events. The last message together with a copy of the "*Chronicle*" I sent with the priest, Father Nikoghayos from Armash, and I believe that with the help of God it did arrive.

On 4 December[5] I departed from the Holy See and went to Akulis. Three or four days later, the khan of Erevan arrived with the *yüz-başı*, the Armenian and Turkish āqās and *kadḵodās*, the *kalāntar* and the melik. We left together from Akulis and on 3 January, we barely reached the hot Moğān Steppe, at a location where the Arax River joins with the Kura River, near Shemakhi, at a distance of one day's travel from it.

---

[1] An official brief. A *kondak* is also a bull, decree, message or epistle of a kat'oghikos.

[2] The *kondak* is only found in Matenadaran MS no. 1387 and in the Vagharshapat edition.

[3] The correct term is the Arabic *maqdasi*, a person who has been on a pilgrimage to Jerusalem.

[4] In the 1870 edition it reads the patriarch of Constantinople.

[5] There is a discrepancy here, for in chapter 22 the date is 3 December. It is possible that Abraham meant the eve of 4 December.

There, in cabins made of reed, on the bank of the Arax, we the poor and pitiful, deprived of all spiritual happiness, celebrated the Birth and Baptism,[1] without a church or a liturgy.

Meanwhile, the almighty Khan, left Tiflis in the direction of the mountains, [fought with] Lesghians and on 11 January victorious arrived at the camp [in the Moğān].

Appearing before him the next day, we congratulated him on his arrival and presented gifts, horses, mules, and that which each one of us had prepared. After he had reassured us, that is, he said, "Welcome! How many days did you travel to get here? How many days have you been here?" He ordered the *dīvān begi*, who was his confidant and relative, saying: "Give the Caliph-baba a good place, so that he is settled." He said to me, "You are excused, caliph," that is you are free, to go to your quarters and rest, do not worry about anything.

After that, day in and day out people arrived from all over: from faraway Ḵorāsān, from Herāt, from Mazandārān, from Mašhad, from the direction of Canaan, from Bākū, from Ardebīl, Azerbaijan, Georgia, Tabrīz, and other places. They arrived, gathered, and congregated there until their *bayram*.

The wise khan determined that every day, three hours after sunrise, everyone would queue and appear before him for the *salām*. Near his living quarters he placed long reed huts, ten, fifteen, and twenty girths in length and two girths in width. Men from each city would sit together with their fellow citizens in one of these huts. We all went to our appropriate places early in the morning and waited there. At the third hour the almighty Khan would come out from his rooms. After the *çāvūş* conducted the prayer, all would go in turn and pass before him, bowing their heads and silently saluting him, and exited.

The place where the Khan sat in state was constructed from wooden logs, the roof was covered with boards and the fence was made of reeds, as were the apartments of his wives. A reed fence surrounded the wall and the residence. There were also many tents.

[1]The Armenian Church celebrates the two events in the same day.

But our quarters were located on the side of the camp, half an hour's ride away. There were some 500 cottages there. They had planned to put some of the khans there, but since they [the cottages] were far from the Khan's residence they were not permitted to do so. Instead they were housed in the vicinity of the Khan's residence.

The Moğān Steppe is a wide, spacious, and splendid plain. A good horseman could not circle it in thirty days. It is flat all over and if one puts an apple on the ground it can be seen from afar. In this boundless plain there are no stones and no evidence of stones. In December and January a plush grass makes the plain green and the sheep have given birth to many lambs. Many of the lambs are grown, as happens in your regions in the days of *khıdrellez*. But it was also very cold and we suffered terribly from it. If there had been no firewood by the banks of the Arax, we would have all been ill and would have died.

On the day of *'arif*, they pitched a large tent, which they had taken the trouble to bring from Qazvīn, inside the reed fence of the Khan's court. The length of the tent was 110 *halebi*, the width 50 *halebi*, and the height 18 *halebi*. It had dome-like tops and was supported by 20 beams. On each beam there was a silver clamp (fastenings), resembling a medium-size watermelon with a sign which was like🡇. The outer covering of the tent was of a dark purple color. The tent was upholstered in two layers. The outside layer was of solid linen on the outer side and wooden railings on the inner side. The inside layer was made of embroidered Gīlān silk.

The great Khan ordered all to go and see the tent. We also went, entered the tent and amused ourselves.

The day of their *bayram* [the great Khan] organized a *maǰlis* (council) of his notables in that tent. The Ottoman Ganǰ 'Alī Pasha, who was the envoy of the Sarakina,[1] as well as the Russian envoy, that is the ambassador from Moscow, were also present in the tent. They invited me to be present as well. They spoke whatever came to their mind.

---

[1]From the Saray, that is the palace of the grand vizier in Istanbul.

Rose water was then distributed and after that sweet sherbet in golden goblets. They walked around those present, spreading incense from two golden and two silver censers. Various *gusans*, among them dancers, who were the humblest of children, performed for an hour. After that we took leave and went to our quarters.

The next day, as customary, we again attended the *salām*. They did not take us to him [however]. Instead they said, “Let each one of you with his fellow citizens sit in the field for we have to present certain orders to you.”

After some time seven noted khans arrived and calling the various groups from each city in turn said, “The great Khan has ordered that you go and consult each other and find someone who could rule over you and the country, for I am tired and weak [said the Khan] and cannot tolerate the pressure of war. I shall go and settle in my fortress and shall pray for you. You have three hours. Consult and return with your answer at the ninth hour.

They then let us go and we returned to our quarters.

At the ninth hour, and even earlier for our own safety, we hurriedly went and once more sat in groups until the same seven men arrived and asked the inhabitants of each city, “Who did you find?” Or else “Did you elect someone?” All answered, “We did not find anyone who was better, more fortunate, or talented than the Khan, and we do not want to search further. If he desires to leave us we shall embrace his feet and become the floor for his clothes. He is our patriarch and is obliged to rule [over us], for he has saved us from our enemies and has wiped the land from evildoers. He snatched us and our families from the hands of enslavers. We cannot exist without him. If he wishes to desert us and our land let him take us with him to Ḵorāsān or else kill us all."

They gave us leave and we went back to our quarters.

The next day we once again went to the same place of deliberations. The seven men appeared once more and like the previous day they called each group from different cities to their presence and said, “The command of the great Khan is as follows,” “Since you did not allow me to carry out my wishes, in order for me to rule over you, I demand three things:

First, You shall cease to curse 'Omar and 'Osman. In the agreement you shall affirm that you will not utter these curses and shall not resume them so in the future. Attach the curse to the person [who breaks this agreement]. For the reason for conflict between our two people, Ottomans and Persians, is the utterance of these curses. They are not written in our Qur'an, are not commanded by our prophet, and are not in our law. Rather, they are invented by men who are dissolute students of religion (*coft*). Because of this much blood has spilled, prisoners taken, and the land destroyed.

Second, give your vow and affirm in the agreement that if the shah or his sons appear you shall not aid them or give them shelter. If you are found guilty of this you shall be put to death by the sword and your property and that of your family shall be taken.

Third, you will be loyal and after my death, continue to be so toward my children and my family. You will remain sincere, submissive, and shall not rebel [against them]. If you break your promise you shall deserve death. You must affix your oath to this."

All unanimously avowed and obligated themselves to carry out the conditions.

They gave us leave and we returned to our quarters.

They then wrote the agreement, amending it repeatedly, until such time when the agreement was acceptable to the mightiest Khan. All the notables from each city affixed their seals to the agreement. From some cities 50, from others 30, 20, 10, from some more, from some less [signature seals]. They [the Khan's men] concluded the agreement and took it with them. Thus everything was accomplished and concluded. After ten days he shall start his rule and the *ǰulūs* will be concluded. This is on account of the dies and the seals, the handles of which are not yet ready. He awaits the completion of the dies and seals.

There is a rumor that he does not wish to be called shah. He has abolished the title of shah all over and no one can mention the title of shah, or call him shah or the previous ruler by that name. He has ordered that they call him *Valīne'mat.*[1]

On one side of the coin is the *tura*[2] resembling a little golden *fndkh.*[3] In the middle of it is the name Nāder, while on the other side of the coin is the [name] of the city where it was minted.

It seems that either today or tomorrow will send the pasha's envoy, that is Ganǰ 'Alī Pasha, together with 'Abd ol-Baqi Khan, to the Sultan. May the God, the Lord, deem that this affair ends well. Amen!

After that [the *Valīne'mat*] began to present in order, *k̲al'ats* to the khans who were present, beginning with the khans from K̲orāsān and ending with the khans of Azerbaijan, after that to those from the Erevan province.

Although a month ago he had sent me two omophorions and one pouch (I think that it was brought from Georgia),[4] and one of the omophorions was very expensive and cost fifty *tomāns*, and even more, while the other one was worth one-third of that. Nevertheless on the day of the meeting when the turn of the Erevanis came, he sent to me via his servants a *k̲al'at*, which was a black but expensive kerchief, a heavy golden-weave *qabā*, and a heavy Circassian girdle. They brought them to my quarters. Many were thus robed with *k̲al'at*. I think they distributed more than 1,000 *k̲al'ats*.

They put on their *k̲al'ats* within three days at the most and presented themselves during the *salām*.

Seeing me, [the *Valīne'mat*] smiled and said to his grandees, " I doubted whether the caliph would tie the kerchief to his head, for he never removes his black cowl from his head." When he saw that I had tied the kerchief to my cowl he was very pleased and said, "How beautiful! How it suits the black on the head."

Three days later he gave us leave and permitted all to go back to their regions. All dispersed full of great admiration.

---

[1]Not substantiated by Persian sources.

[2]*Ṭuğrā*, an emperor's seal, usually written in fine ornamental script.

[3]Persian *fandoq*, Turkish *fındık*, which is a filbert or hazelnut. *Fındık altını* was also the name of a Turkish gold coin.

[4]Parentheses in the original.

May everything come to a good end, with the help of God! Amen!

Written on the Moğān on 20 February in the year 1175 (1736). And thus on the 24th day of the moon [the *Valīne'mat*] shall ascend the throne, for the dies and the seals for the coins are ready. I am enclosing samples of the inscriptions in this message, so that no one will have any doubts. Enough has been said.

Inscription on the Coin

Sekke'i bezar kard nām-e salṭanat rā dar ǰahān,
Šāh-e dīn Nāder Qolī Eskandar-e ṣāḥebqerān.[1]
He announces his reign to the world by striking gold (coin)
King of faith, Nāder Qolī, invincible as Alexander

Inscription on the Seal (*mohr*)

Nagīn-e dowlat va dīn rafte būd čon azǰā,
Benām-e Nāder-e Irān qarār dād ḵodā.[2]
Since the ring of state and religion had vanished from its place
God reinstated it in the name of the Iranian Nāder

***Fateḥlame* (*Fatḥnāme*)**[3]
Pādešāh-e mamālek-e Īrān żell-e sobḥān Nāder-e dowrān.[4]
King of the Iranian lands, shadow of God, wonder of our age

Fathi (Fāteḥ) " The Conqueror"[5]

[1]The text is in Persian written in Armenian letters.
[2]The text is in Persian written in Armenian letters.
[3]The announcement of victory.
[4]The text is in Persian written in Armenian letters.
[5]Abraham flatters Nāder by using the title of the Ottoman sultan, Mehmet II (*Fathi*).

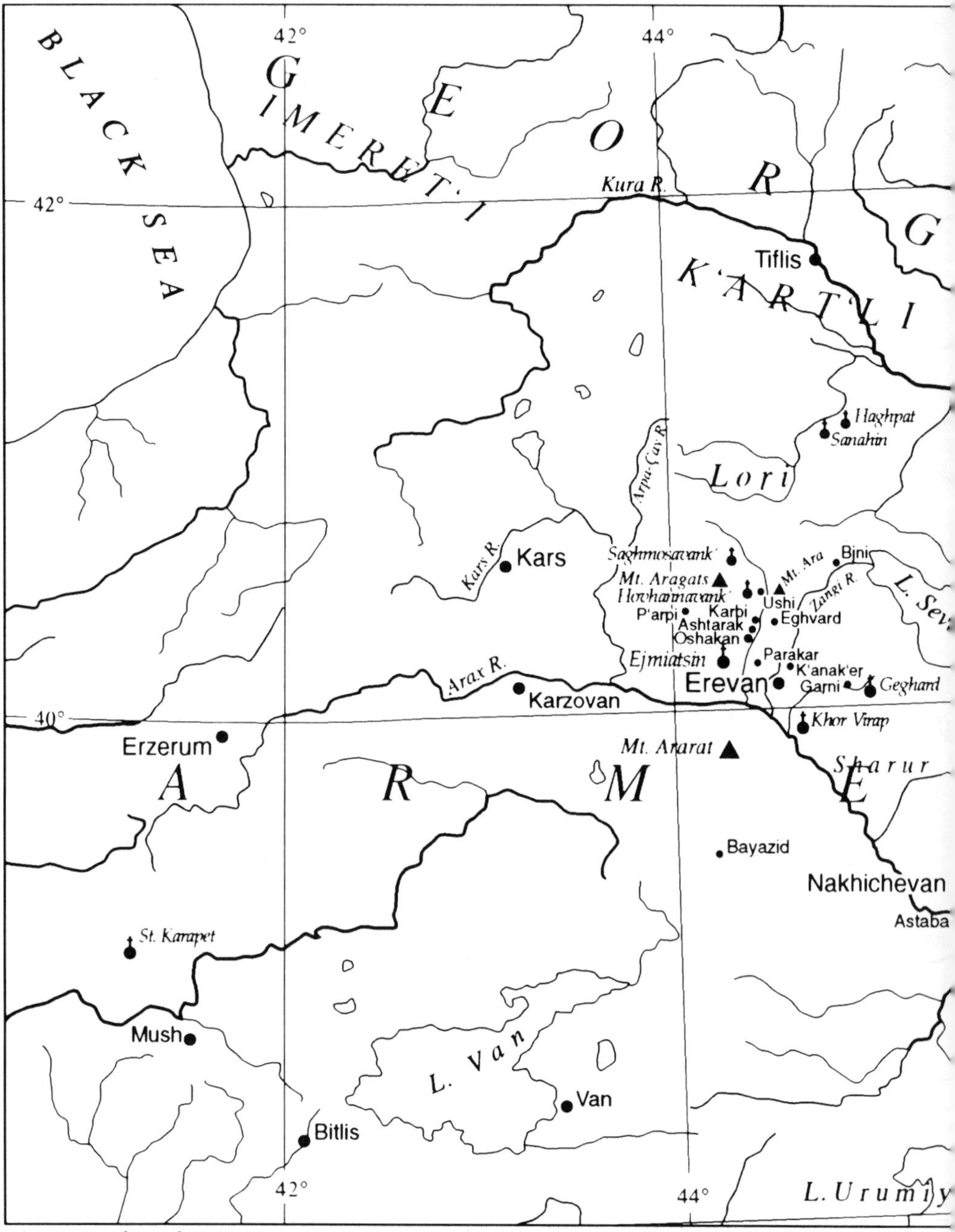

Geographical Locations mentioned in the text

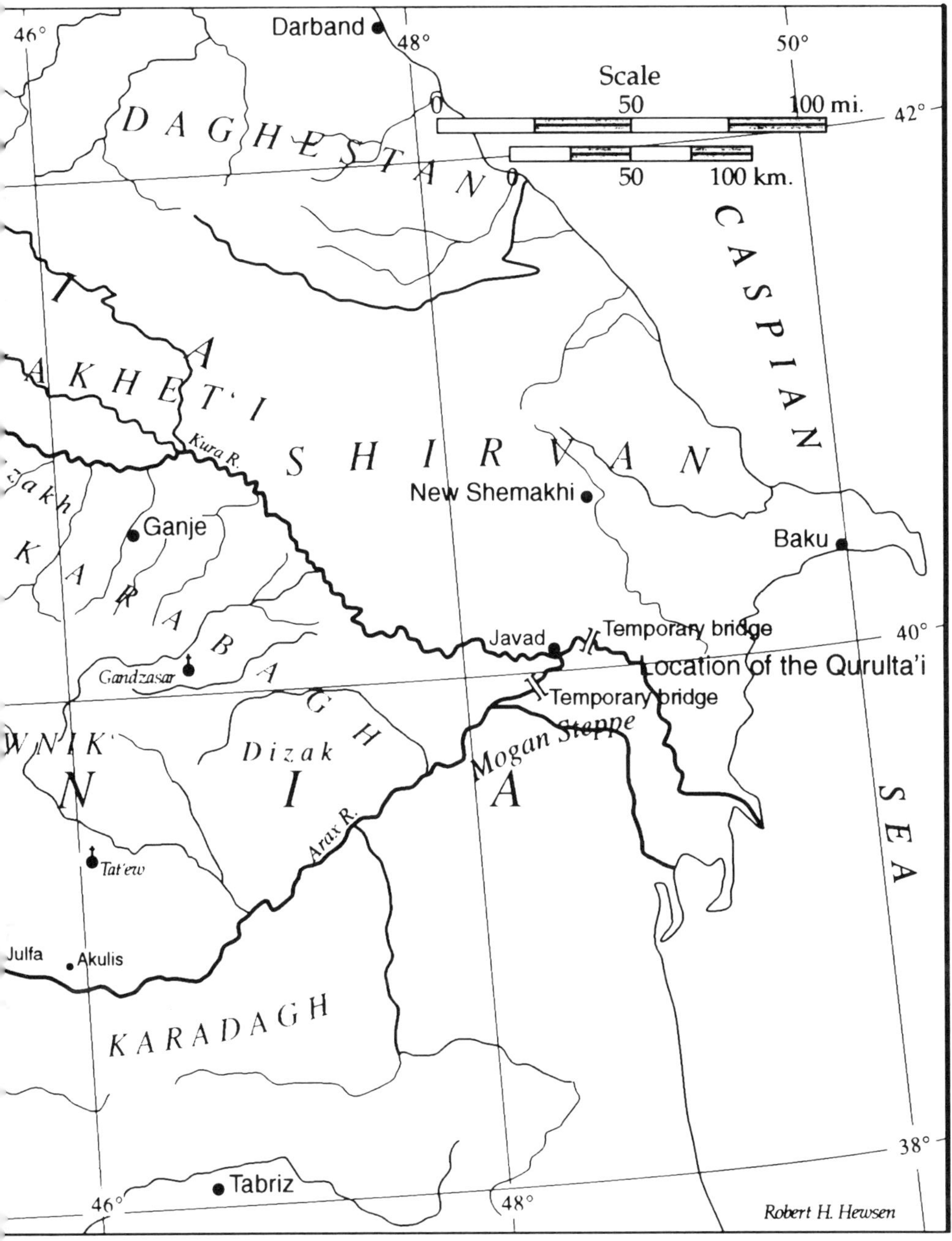

Darband
46°
48°
50°
Scale
0
50
100 mi.
42°
0
50
100 km.
DAGHESTAN
CASPIAN
KAKHET'I
Kura R.
SHIRVAN
New Shemakhi
Ganje
Baku
KARABAGH
Javad
Temporary bridge
40°
Location of the Qurulta'i
Gandzasar
Temporary bridge
Mogan Steppe
Dizak
N
I
A
Arax R.
SEA
Tat'ew
Julfa
Akulis
KARADAGH
38°
Tabriz
46°
48°
Robert H. Hewsen

Commentary

The *Chronicle* of Abraham of Crete is one of the few non-Persian primary sources on the events that occurred in Transcaucasia and northwestern Iran during the years 1734-1736.[1] We can only speculate on Abraham's motive in writing the *Chronicle*. His primary audience was certainly the hierarchy of the Holy See. It is very probable that his old age and ill health prompted him to record the promises, privileges, and property rights granted by the new Persian administration to Ējmiatsin, orally and through various decrees. Such a record would have been of great use to his successors. It is interesting to note, however, that Abraham sent a detailed summary of the *Chronicle* to the Armenian Church hierarchy in the Ottoman Empire, as well. We can only surmise as to why. Perhaps, it was in order to provide the Patriarchate in Istanbul with evidence that would persuade the Sublime Porte to grant it similar *raqams*. It may also have been to establish a record in those uncertain times of Persian respect for the Holy See, in the event that the Turks returned to Ējmiatsin.

[1]The two other Armenian sources are by Abraham of Erevan, which describes the various wars which took place in the region from 1721 to 1736 and by Hakob of Shemakhi, which lacks the detail and accuracy of the *Chronicle* (see bibliography). A number of European sources, mainly those written by James Fraser, Jean Otter, Louis André de la Mamye-Clairac, Jonas Hanway, the Jesuit father, Louis Bazin, and several anonymous authors, lack the necessary information as well. These authors either, never met Nāder, never came to Iran, gathered their information from second-hand sources or "well-informed persons," or witnessed the events prior to 1734 or after 1737 (see bibliography).

The only other contemporary sources that match Abraham's *Chronicle* in detail and accuracy are in Persian.[1] The first is *J̌ahāngošāy-e Nāderī* (also known as *Tārīḵ-e Nāderī*) by Mīrzā Moḥammad Mahdī Khan Kowkabī Astarābādī. The author was first a scribe in the royal secretariat of Ṭahmāsp (ca. 1726). By 1730 he had become chief secretary (*monšī al-mamālek*), and after 1736, the official historiographer of Nāder. He served in this capacity, as well as performing other court duties, until Nāder's death in 1747. A critical edition of his history, under the direction of 'Abdollāh Anvār, appeared in Tehran in 1962.

The second is *'Ālam-ārāy-e Nāderī* (also known as *Name-ye ālām-ārā-ye Nāderī*, *Nāder-Nāme*, or *Ketāb-e Nāderī*) by Moḥammad Kāżem Marvī. The author was in the service of Nāder's brother, Ebrāhīm, in Tabrīz, and by 1740 had joined Nāder's secretariat. He also served there until the end of Nāder's life. The only existing manuscript of Moḥammad Kāżem's history is at the Oriental Institute of the Academy of Sciences in St. Petersburg, Russia (MS no. D 430). A facsimile edition of that manuscript, with introductions by the noted scholar N. D. Miklukho-Maklai, was published in three volumes in Moscow (1960-1966). It was only in 1990 that a three-volume printed edition prepared by Moḥammad Amīn Riyāḥī was published in Tehran.

Although much of Abraham's narrative is substantiated by both of these Persian sources, there are two differences worth noting: First, there is no mention in either of the Persian sources of any of Kat'oghikos Abraham's numerous meetings and conversations with Nāder, noted with such detail in the *Chronicle*. Mīrzā Mahdī

[1]Moḥammad Ḥosein Qodūsī's *Nāder-nāme* does not offer any additional information on the period covered by Abraham, while Sheikh Moḥammad 'Alī Ḥazīn's *Tarīḵ-e Ḥazīn* (*Tazkirat al-aḥvāl*) covers earlier events. Ḵ'āje 'Abdol-Karīm Kašmīrī's *Bayān-e Vāqe'* and Moḥammad Šafī''s *Tārīke-e Nāderšāhī* both concentrate on Nāder in India. Finally Mīrzā Mahdī's other work on Nāder, *Dorreh-ye Nāderi*, a verbose book, full of Arabic words, adds little to his first account, as is the case with a number of anonymous monographs (see bibliography).

is totally silent on Nāder's visit to Ējmiatsin, described so vividly by Abraham. Although Moḥammad Kāżem refers to Nāder's visit to Ējmiatsin, there is no mention of Abraham. Furthermore, Moḥammad Kāżem states that the visit took place after the battle of Eghvard and not, as Abraham states, prior to it. He adds that Nāder visited the cloister for the sake of Melik Egan, the secular chief of the Armenians in Azerbaijan, who had performed valuable services at the siege of Ganǰe, as well as to please the Russian empress. He notes that Nāder presented the priests at Ējmiatsin with golden candelabras and valuable gifts before going on to Tiflis,[1] whereas Abraham specifically states that Nāder presented the Holy See with a bag of gold florins.[2]

Second, and more significantly, there is no indication of Abraham's presence at the *qurulta'i* in the Persian sources. There is no doubt that Abraham was present at the gathering on the Moǧān, for his account, written several years prior to that of Mīrzā Mahdī's or Moḥammad Kāżem's histories, details the same dates and events described by them. One can assume that either Nāder's extremely favorable attitude toward the Christian leader was not worth noting to these Muslim historians; or that Abraham's view of his relations with Nāder was insignificant to them compared to the major events which took place at the time.

Each of the three chroniclers describes certain events not mentioned by the other two; taken together they present a more complete account of events of the period. Abraham's description of the battle of Eghvard curiously omits the role of the Armenians in that conflict. According to Mīrzā Mahdī, following the death of 'Abdullah Pasha:

> *A number of companies of [Turkish] troops fled towards Üç-Kilisa, Karpi (Kaṛbi), and Ashtarak. The Armenians villagers of these districts (mahāl) blocked their way by the gorge of Ashtarak. The Armenians with club and stones from one direction*

---

[1]Moḥammad Kāżem, *op.cit.*, I, f. 311b (Moscow facsimile edition) or I, 411 (Tehran edition).

[2]See Chapter XI.

and the [Persian] brave soldiers with guns and bullets from the other, killed some three to four thousand men whose horses stampeded and threw them to their death into the deep gorge.[1]

Moḥammad Kāżem, in turn, describes an interesting episode, which is absent from both Mīrzā Mahdī's and Abraham's narratives. In order to test the true feelings of the Persian nobles toward his elevation to the position of shah, Nāder invited them to great banquets where there was a great deal to drink. After four days of such drunken merrymaking, no one made an unflattering comment. The *mulla-başı*, Mīrzā ʻAbd ol-Ḥasan, however, was overheard, in the privacy of his tent, expressing support for the Ṣafavids. The next day he was strangled in Nāder's presence, after which, Moḥammad Kāżem writes, no one dared to oppose Nāder.[2]

Abraham is the only source which states that Nāder demanded two additional conditions prior to his acceptance of the crown. The first was the rejection of any member of the Ṣafavid family who might appear in the future. The second was loyalty to his dynasty after his death.[3]

Mīrzā Mahdī mentions the undisputed and very significant fact, that Nāder, prior to his coronation, made those present agree to his sending an embassy to the Sultan in Constantinople in order to negotiate peace on the basis of the following points:

1) Since the Persians had given up their former belief [Shiʻism] and chosen the religion of the Ottomans [Sunni Islam], they were to be recognized as a fifth sect [the *J̌aʻfarī]* of Islam.

2) Since each of the imams of the four existing sects had a column in the Kaʻba, another column [fifth] was to be erected for the *J̌aʻfarīs* in Mecca.

3) A Persian *amir al-Haǰ* [leader of the Pilgrimage to Mecca], whose position would be equivalent to that of the *amir al-Haǰ* of

[1]Mīrzā Mahdī, *op.cit.*, p. 255. Moḥammad Kāżem does not mention the role of the Armenians.

[2]Kazem, op. cit., II, 455 (Tehran edition).

[3]See Chapter XXXV.

Egypt and Syria (Šām), would be appointed annually and would be permitted by the Ottomans to lead the Persian pilgrims [to Mecca].

4) An exchange of prisoners would take place and none would be bought or sold.

5) A representative (*vakīl*) from each state would reside at the capital of the other.

'Alī Pasha, the former governor of Ganǰe (hence Ganǰ 'Ali Pasha in the *Chronicle*), who was the Ottoman envoy at the Moğān, took these conditions along with lavish gifts, accompanied by Persian representatives, to Constantinople. Although the Ottomans accepted the last three points, they refused to accept the first two. An agreement encompassing the last three points was drawn and sent to Nāder and the state of war was officially suspended.

The agreement was never ratified, however. It is possible that Nāder was simply buying time until he was ready to crush the Ottomans completely. Lockhart suggests that his rejection of Shi'ism was not genuine, but was intended to make him more acceptable as the supreme ruler of the entire Muslim world—after he had conquered Delhi and Constantinople.[1]

By the summer of 1743 Nāder, having defeated the Mughals, received the news that the Ottomans still refused to accept the first two points of his proposal. He prepared for war. After some initial victories in Mesopotamia, a stalemate ensued. Revolts in Iran and Daghestan forced Nāder to send proposals of peace. When the Porte rejected his offer Nāder was furious and advanced on Transcaucasia. A number of battles were fought around Kars, Akhalk'alak'i and Akhaltsikhe. The Georgians led by T'eimuraz and Erekle helped the Persians and were awarded K'art'li and Kakhet'i for their services.[2]The decisive battle was fought on 11 August 1745 in the field of Eghvard, the site of the Turkish defeat a decade before. The Ottomans were once again routed, with many casualties. Realizing that Iran could not sustain a state of continuous warfare, Nāder, after further negotiations, accepted the Treaty of Kur-

[1]Lockhart, *op. cit.*, p. 100.

[2]M. F. Brosset, *Histoire de la Géorgie*, II (pt. I) (St. Petersburg, 1856), 198.

dan (37 miles northwest of Tehran), signed on 4 September 1746),[1] which restored the 1639 borders[2] agreed between the Ṣafavids and the Ottomans.[3]

Abraham is careful to mark many chapters and events by citing the day, the date, or the religious feast and is therefore a valuable source for calculating the precise date of certain events. For example Mīrzā Mahdī gives June 18 (1735) as the day of the battle of Eghvard.[4] The great history of the Ottoman Empire by Hammer has June 14.[5] Abraham's date of June 19,[6] however, is confirmed in a Russian report, as well as in a letter from Nāder to Golitsyn.[7] The *Chronicle* is the only other source that confirms the date of Nāder's arrival on the Moġān[8] recorded by Mīrzā Mahdī as the evening of 22 January 1736.[9] It also confirms the coronation date of 8 March,[10] as recorded by Mīrzā Mahdī,[11] versus Hanway's incorrect date of 22 March.[12] The *Chronicle* also confirms the date of the death of Kat'oghikos Abraham II and the date of his own anointment.

The *Chronicle* is also an important source of information on the political, ecclesiastical, and socioeconomic history of Armenia. Abraham makes it clear that in the absence of a true political leadership, the Muslims grouped their Christian subjects into commu-

---

[1]The text of the treaty is in Hurewitz, op. cit., I, 51-52.

[2]The text of the Treaty of Zuhab is in *Ibid.*, I, 21-23.

[3]The twelve-year Russo-Turkish invasion and occupation of Transcaucasia and northern Iran, which resulted in more than 100,000 casualties from war and disease with the restoration of the pre-1722 borders. The Ottomans sent magnificent gifts, including a throne and a bejeweled dagger, to Iran. Nāder's never saw the gifts, and his assassination, prior to the arrival of the Turkish embassy, resulted in their return. Today they are in the Topkapi Palace Museum.

[4]Mīrzā Mahdī, *op. cit.* p. 254.

[5]Hammer, *op. cit.*, XIV, 337.

[6]See Chapter XIV.

[7]Lockhart, p. 88, n. 4.

[8]See Chapter XXIV.

[9]Mīrzā Mahdī, *op. cit.*, p. 267.

[10]See Chapter XLIII.

[11]Mīrzā Mahdī, *op. cit.* p. 271.

[12]Hanway, *op. cit.*, IV, 127.

nities administered by their religious leaders. In fact, the Ottomans and the Persians both address Abraham as the "caliph" of the Armenians.

During the seventeenth century, Ṣafavid protection and the wealth of the Armenian merchant class in New Julfa, as well as the inclusion of the Holy See of Ējmiatsin within the Persian realm (after the treaty of 1639), gave Armenian religious and lay leaders in Persia and Transcaucasia the opportunity to have a major voice in the election of the kat'oghikos.[1]The collapse of the Ṣafavids, however, put an end to Persian Armenian influence. The fall of Isfahan and the looting of New Julfa by the Afghans, the Ottoman invasion of Transcaucasia and northern Persia, the sudden death of Kat'oghikos Astuatsatur (1715-1725), the end of active Russian involvement in the region following the death of Peter the Great, and the inability of the Persians to regain the region, forced the Ējmiatsin hierarchy to rely on the Armenians of Constantinople for political support. The Turkish Armenian religious and lay leaders began, therefore, to assume a major role in the election of the kat'oghikos.[2]The Ottoman sultans not only confirmed the choice of their Armenian subjects with official decrees, but also maintained the tax-exempt status of the Holy See. Following the death of Abraham, the Armenians of Constantinople maintained their firm hold on the election of the supreme patriarch until the start of the nineteenth century, when the Persians and especially the Russians involved themselves in the election process.[3]

The issue of the control of and responsibility for the funds of the Holy See and its various dioceses in Transcaucasia and northern Iran, is addressed when Abraham describes how he had to borrow money for expenses and had to carry some funds to purchase provisions, horses, mules, camels and fodder.[4]Moneylenders, both Armenian and Muslim, did business with the leadership of the Ar-

---

[1]For more details see, Bournoutian, Russia and the Armenians...*op. cit.*, pp. 456-459.

[2]*Ibid.*

[3]*Ibid.*, pp. 459-461.

[4]See Chapter VIII.

menian Church and made them sign promissory notes. The times of troubles made such transactions necessary and, later, in the nineteenth century, would cause major problems for the Holy See.[1]

The relation of Abraham with the kat'oghikos of Aghuank' is also noteworthy. Although by the nineteenth century, the patriarchs of Gandzasar attempted to gain complete independence from Ējmiatsin,[2] Nersēs seems to have accepted Abraham as his superior. There is also the possibility that Nersēs, not a member of the Hasan Jalalean clan which traditionally held the kat'oghikosate of Aghuank', needed Ējmiatsin's endorsement.[3]

Both the Ottomans and the Persians sought the cooperation of their Armenian subjects, who were significant, numerically and economically. The new pasha of Erevan made this perfectly clear when he stated: "*Manage this cloister, which not only belongs to you [the Armenians], but to our king [the Sultan] as well. We plan to remain here [in this region] and [we] need this place.*"[4]

Nāder is especially fond of Abraham and treats him with great respect. Abraham is seated among the highest-ranking officials and receives magnificent gifts, equaling or surpassing those given to Persian commanders.[5] It is possible that since he had received aid from Armenian meliks of Karabagh and Azerbaijan in a number of past campaigns, he was displaying his gratitude.[6] The presence of a number of Armenian meliks from Erevan and Nakhichevan and their followers in Nāder's army might have been another reason.[7] The fact that Abraham spoke Turkish and was a natural-born diplomat must have helped as well. Nāder's negotiations with Russia also necessitated an image of a tolerant ruler. Nor can the economic contribution of the Armenians be ignored. Finally, Nāder

[1]See Bournoutian, Khanate of Erevan , op. cit., pp. 65-92.

[2]See Bournoutian, Russia and the Armenians...*op, cit.*, docs. 110, 144.

[3]The Hasan Jalaleans did not always acknowledge Ējmiatsin. This was especially true in the late eighteenth and early nineteenth centuries. The Russians abolished that kat'oghikosate in 1815.

[4]See Chapter VII.

[5]See Chapters XXVI, XXXIII, and XXXVIII.

[6]Mīrzā Kāżem, *op. cit.*, I, 441.

[7]See Chapters X, XIII.

was planning to ascend the throne and wished to emulate the Ṣafavids. Since they, despite occasional extortion, had granted special privileges to the Armenians, Nāder may have felt it necessary to follow suit. It must be noted that Nāder's friendliness toward Abraham and some Armenian officials was not indicative of his behavior towards every Armenian. Numerous Armenians were taken hostage and had to pay exorbitant sums to escape persecution or forcible emigration, as indicated by the action of the Armenians of Tiflis.[1] Despite his praises of Nāder, Abraham's text clearly implies that he and others around Nāder constantly feared for their lives. Nāder's cruelty and tyranny, which became out of control a decade later and led to his murder, manifested itself occasionally during this period. The threat of death hung continuously over Nāder's guards and close advisors as well. It is not surprising that every time Abraham left Nāder's presence he thanked God for his safe return.

Abraham's predecessor not only took him to visit several monasteries, but also sent him to inspect others. It is possible that having no other suitable candidate, Abraham II focused on the author of the *Chronicle* as his possible successor. Abraham's unfamiliarity with the region, for the most part, gave him the opportunity to provide the reader with interesting geographical details. The *Chronicle* describes numerous monasteries and Armenian settlements in the Araratian region as well as in Karabagh.[2] Despite the difficulties of travel and the political uncertainties, Abraham made it clear that he made it his duty to visit the various dioceses and churches to ascertain their economic and spiritual condition. Considering the age and health of the various kat'oghikoi, such visits must have been extremely tiring with the poor hygienic conditions which promoted disease and death.

---

[1]See Chapter XIX.

[2]Unfortunately Abraham was not aware of, or chose not to discuss, the Armenian resistance against the Turkish invaders in Zangezur and Karabagh, which had occurred several years before his arrival, see History of Dawit' Beg in Brosset, *op. cit.*, II, 223-255.

The *Chronicle* provides a valuable description of the terrible economic conditions in eastern Armenia and northern Iran at this time. A region known for its rich agricultural output and trade during much of the seventeenth century had sunk into poverty. The Ottoman occupation from 1723 to 1735 and the arbitrary taxation, as well as extortion, by some Turkish governors, had left its scars.[1] Moreover, the wars between the Ottomans and Persians, which resulted in the requisitioning of food and animals, left many villages and peasants destitute.[2] The supply of coins became so low as to virtually disappear.[3] Trade had to be encouraged and solicited.[4] The shortage of food even forced some of Nāder's guests, including Abraham, to depart early and miss his coronation.[5] Finally, corruption and bribery by local officials added to the misery of the population.[6] Abraham made it clear that he could discern flattering hypocritical Muslim officials from sincere ones.[7] The unspecified epidemic (probably cholera or typhus) which spread throughout the Araratian region in the late summer of 1734, and carried off many Armenians, Persians, and Turks (including Kat'oghikos Abraham II and the Pasha of Erevan) is mentioned prominently in the *Chronicle*, but is not described in the Persian sources.[8]

The Ṣafavid practice of forcibly depopulating eastern Armenia and removing its productive people to the interior of Iran was revived under Nāder. He ordered that 6,000 Armenian farmers and artisans from eastern Anatolia[9] and 300 Armenian families from the Erevan region be moved to Ḵorāsān, to bolster the economy of his home province.[10]

---

[1]See Chapter III.
[2]See Chapter XII.
[3]See Chapter XX.
[4]*Ibid.*
[5]See Chapter XLII.
[6]See Chapter LI.
[7]See Chapter LII.
[8]See Chapters V-VI.
[9]See Chapter XVII.
[10]See Chapter XIX.

The destruction of the town of Shemakhi has not been described in many sources. Sometime in the spring of 1735 (probably early April) Nāder, during the siege of Ganǰe, dispatched troops to check the Lesghians invaders from Daghestan from making inroads into Shirvan. It must have been at this time that he decided to destroy Shemakhi, and move most of its inhabitants to Aq Su, some fifteen miles to the southwest. Although his excuse was that the city was too open to attack, the real cause seems to have been the aid given to the Lesghians by the town, which was thus punished. Turkish prisoners were used to help construct the new site, which was named New Shemakhi. The *Chronicle* not only mentions the move, but also states that the destruction occurred in two stages. It describes the difficulties of the Armenians of Shemakhi, the increase of their poll tax and the harassment by the local tribes, about which they complained to Abraham and on account of which he asked Nāder for a *raqam* designating a separate quarter for the Armenians.[1]

A unique piece of information, not detailed in both Persian sources, concerns Abraham's purchasing of Armenian prisoners. Despite Nāder's claims to safeguard the Christians, he took 7000 captives—a mixed group of Armenians and Georgians—from eastern Georgia. He distributed half of them to the delegates present on the Moğān. from among the population of eastern Armenia and eastern Georgia. A large number of men, boys, and women, some pregnant, were redeemed by Abraham.[2]Some were just too expensive to keep and were given free to Abraham, others may have been presented to him in consideration of Nāder's favor towards him. Although unlikely, Abraham, in order to protect their honor, makes it a point to assure the reader that all the pregnant Armenian women among the captives had been impregnated by their husbands prior to their capture.[3]

---

[1]See Chapter XLII. The poll tax remained a problem in that region up to the 19th century see, Bournoutian, Russia and the Armenians…*op. cit.* doc. 169.

[2]See Chapter XXXVIII.

[3]See Chapter XLII.

Abraham was well aware of the importance of official documents and royal edicts in times of uncertainty. He constantly asked for various *raqams* attesting to a tax-exempt status or to the jurisdiction of the Church over Armenian villages. He is careful to obtain them not only from Nāder,[1] but also from his brother, Ebrāhīm, who became the governor of the entire region.[2] Land deeds and other privileges which were granted the Armenian Church beginning with the Ilkhanids and continuing throughout the Aq Qoyunlu, Qara Qoyunlu, and Ṣafavid periods[3] were thus reaffirmed by Nāder.[4]

One of the most interesting facts mentioned in the *Chronicle* is the presence of Armenian, Greek, Albanian, and Bosnian troops in the Ottoman army.[5] Although the Albanians and Bosnians were probably converts to Islam, the presence of Armenians and Greeks among the troops is noteworthy. It is true that all non-Muslim adult males paid the *jizya* and generally did not serve in the army. However, sources indicate that non-Muslim inhabitants of frontier districts, could, at certain times, be enrolled in military expeditions, and could be released from the payment of *jizya* for the year. Therefore, the Armenians and Greeks were either converts, were recruited in exchange for the exemption from the *jizya*, or were punished for the non-payment of that tax.

Since the Persian primary sources have only a few pages on the *qurulta'i* (national council),[6] the *Chronicle's* sixty-five pages (twenty-three chapters out of the fifty-three chapters of the book), which are devoted entirely to this event, provide a wealth of material for the historians of Iran. No other source provides such details on the *qurulta'i*. The different accommodations; the food and

---

[1]See Chapter XXXIX.

[2]See Chapter LI.

[3]The earliest Persian document is an Ilkhanid land grant dated 1305, see P'ap'azyan, Land Deeds, *op. cit.*, pp. 405-411.

[4]The Qājārs continued this tradition, see Bournoutian, Khanate of Erevan, *op. cit.*, pp. 65-92.

[5]See Chapters XIV-XV.

[6]Mīrzā Mahdī, *op. cit.* pp. 266-274; Moḥammad Kāẓem, *op. cit.*, pp. 446-458.

drinks; the music, musicians, and type of instruments; the various dancers and tight-rope walkers; the daily audiences; the elaborate process of making Nāder the choice of the assembled grandees; the description of troops and attendants, their arms and clothing; the comprehensive list of the delegates and guests; the types and value of the numerous *k̲al'ats*, the physical description of the Moğān, the temporary bridges across the Arax and the Kura; and the entire coronation ceremony are all vividly described. The *Chronicle* is also one of the few sources which identifies the secular Armenian leaders of eastern Armenia and enumerates their duties.

It is important to note that the Muslims showed an interest, perhaps even a respect verging on superstition, for certain aspects of Armenian religious practices. They anointed themselves with the *meṛon* and unhesitatingly entered the cathedral of Ējmiatsin to hear Abraham speak. Nāder also asked Abraham to pray for him.[1] It is probable that most Muslims felt that the strong presence and stature of the Armenian Church and its hierarchy, as well as relics such as the Holy Spear, could intercede on their behalf before God.

Finally, the *Chronicle* is a unique source for those interested in the uses of languages in the period and the region. In addition to the eighteenth-century Armenian, the text abounds with phrases and terms in Persian, Ottoman, Arabic, Kurdish, Mongol, and Azeri.[2] Officials' titles and duties, items of food, utensils, and clothing, troops, taxes, weights, measures, housing, religious terms, and the daily vocabulary are used interchangeably in half a dozen languages. Since Abraham was confident that his readers would recognize these terms, it is certain that the Persian, Kurdish, Georgian, Arab, Turkish, and Mongol languages had not only spread throughout historic Armenia (eastern Anatolia, northwestern Azerbaijan, and western Transcaucasia), but had developed into a dialect which was a combination of all these various languages.

---

[1] See Chapters XVI, XXIII and LIII.

[2] See glossary of non-Armenian terms.

Glossary of non-Armenian Terms[1]

ābādān: cultivated, plentiful
alay: troops in line during a procession
amīrāḵor: horse master
ambārdār: keeper of the provisions
amrdolu (amlordvi): son of the barren woman (John the Baptist)
āqā (ağa in Turkish*)*: notable, supervisor, master.
'arif: The last day of *Ramadhan.*
arya: Persian
'arza ('arze): petition
aşçı-başı: head cook
ašrafī: gold coin worth five *tomāns*
'ašūrā: martyrdom of Imam Ḥosein on the tenth day of Muharram in Karbala.
'ayān: notables

bādeh: bowl
bahra (*bahreh*): taxes on crops; share of the lord
bālāpūš: overcoat
bali (bale): yes; at your service
bayram: religious festival
bāzrgān-başı: head of merchants, privy-treasurer
beglarbegi: governor general
borazan: trumpet
bostanci-basi: roadway and canal guards
buḵurdar: censer
buyrutlu: mandate

[1]The definitions reflect the contemporary meaning of the terms in the region, some of which changed over time.

buyur: command me; what is your wish; at your service
buyutāt: craftsmen employed by the *dīvān* or the court.

čādor (çadir): tent
čandāvul: rear guard
čāpār: courier
čārḵečī: advance troops
čāšīdan: to taste various foods
çavuş: halberdier
čerkes: Circassian
chyrnykh: wooden launch
cibinlik: mosquito net
coft: student of religion
čogān (cuygan): club; an arched pole to which an iron ball is suspended and carried as an ensign of royalty.
čol (*çöl*): arid plain
čomāq: mace
čoqedār: lackey

daftar (*defter*): office, registry, notebook
damad: son-in-law
defterdar (*daftardār*): commissary general of a province or keeper of financial records
defter-emini: person in charge of land registry
dīvān: chancery
dīvānḵāne: audience hall
donluk: clothing and money allotments to the troops
došak: mattress
dram: small coin, a *dinar*, a *drachma*, a *dirham*; measure of weight equal to one-eight of an ounce
du'ā: prayer

elāğājlī: sons of khans
elçi (īlčī): envoy, ambassador
elli-başı: head of 50 men

'eyvān: veranda

falake: bastinado
farmān: royal decree
farmān-ravā: ruler
farrāš: chamberlain
fāteḥ: conqueror
fatihat: opening lines of the Qur'an
fatwa: judicial decree
fener (fanar): lantern
findik (*fandoq*): filbert, hazelnut
florin: large silver coin

ğarīb: stranger
gaz: A measure of length equal to a yard or cubit
gümüş: silvery
gusan: troubadour

ḥāǰǰi: one who has performed the *ḥaǰǰ* or pilgrimage to Mecca
ḥalebi: a measure of cloth equaling 20 to 30 inches
hamīše: permanent
hıdrellez (ḵezẹrlez): fortieth day after the spring equinox
ḥisāb: accounts

'ibqā': to preserve
'Id ul-Fiṭr: celebration marking the end of *Ramadhan*
ilakha: state income
irat (irad): expenses

ǰānbāz: acrobat
ǰārčī (ǰārǰī): messenger, herald, town crier
ǰašn: feast, banquet
ǰazāyir: large musket fired on a stand
ǰazāyirčī: musketeers using a large musket

ǰīqe (ǰeqe): adornments of plumes worn on head gear rulers, as well as high-ranking officers
ǰulūs: accession

k̲abar: news, information
kābīn: marriage contract
kadk̲odā (*kekhia*): community elder, head of village or quarter
kalāntar: official who acted as a mayor, coroner, and constable
k̲al'at (pl. *k̲ila'*): honor conferred by princes upon subjects consisting of turban, robe, and girdle
k̲alīfe (*k̲alifa*): caliph
kamānce: a small string instrument
kamk̲ā: rare silk
kanava: canvas
kanun: a zither-like instrument
k̲ānzādeh: son of a khan
kapıcı-başı: chief gate-keeper
kāteb: clerk
k̲āṭer: having affection for
keçe-kalpak: felt hat
kešīkčī: guard
kešīk-k̲āne: guard house
kīse: a purse of gold or silver coins
kızılbāş: red cap followers of the Ṣafavids; refers to Muslims in Armenian texts and to Persians in Ottoman texts
kizlar-ağası: chief black eunuch of the harem
komak: aid
k̲owrāk: food, provisions
kuruş: Turkish small coins worth a *piastre*.
kyurdeki: man's jacket

leḥāf: blanket
leyle cadir: night tent for the guards

maga'er: caverns

mahacar kafes: carved woodwork
maḥal: district
maḥẓar: petition or testimony attested by witnesses, muster-roll
maǰlis: council
manqulat: movable property
maqdasi: one who has been on a pilgrimage to Jerusalem
maqrī: one who recites the Qur'an
marz: border
maṣraf: expense, disbursement, receipt
matariz (*matrez*): bastion
ma'yar bašī: assessor of quality and weight of coins
mehmāndār: one who is in charge of receiving and entertaining guests
mehter-kane: band of musicians
mendil: kerchief
millet: a minority supervised by its religious leaders
min-başı: head of a 1000 men
mīrī: state treasury
mīrzā: scribe, secretary, or state official (if preceded a name), prince (if followed a name)
mobāšer (*mubašir*): superintendent
mohrdar: keeper of the seal of a ruler
monšī: scribe, secretary
monšī al-mamālek: chief secretary of the dīvān.
morrak̲aṣ: free to leave
mostowfī: head clerk or controller
mo'tamed: trustworthy
mo'tamin (*mo'tamen*): supervisor of expenses
mu'āf: tax-exempt, exempt
mubārak: auspicious
mufti: magistrate
muḥafiż: defender, guardian, warden
Muharram: the first month of the Islamic lunar calendar
muḥāsib: auditor
mulk (*molk*): private holdings

mulla-başı: chief mulla
muteselim (mutesalim): deputy governor

nāder: rare, wonder
nāderī: silver coin worth 500 *dinars*
na'ib: deputy
namāz: prayer
naqāreh: a drum played with *zurna*
naqāreh-ḵāne: band of musicians
naqš: engraved, painted, decorated
nasaqčī-başı: commander of guards
nāyeb al-salṭane: regent
nokār: servants, armed attendants, militia
nowrūz: Persian New Year (first day of spring)

ocak (*'oǰāq*): house, hearth
okka (*oqqe*): measure of weight equal to 2.83 lbs.
on-başı: head of ten men
orduci: craftsmen who accompany the army
oṭāq: room

pahlavān: wrestler, strong man
parmaklik: banister, railing
parvardegār: God
pashalik: district

qabā: tunic
qabāle: land deed
qadagan: forbidden
qaisar: emperor
qālī (*khali*): fine carpet
qālīče: mat, rug
qalyān: water-pipe
qarnay: flute or trumpet
qaṭīfe: velvet or satin mantle

qāẓī (*qadhi*): judge of the *Šarī'a* court
qonaq (*konak*): guest
qurulta'i: national council

ra'īs: chief, magistrate
raqam: writ, royal order
ra'yat (pl. *ra'āyā*): subjects, non-Muslims, peasants
reyḥān: basil

sādeh: ordinary
ṣāḥeb-e 'ayār: assessor of quality and weight of coins
sāḥebqerān: fortunate, invincible; also a silver coins (later called *qerān*)
šāhī: coin equal to five silver kopeks
šāh-vekīl: district supervisor
sā'is: master of horse
salām: audience granted by a ruler
ṣanduqdār: treasurer, keeper of privy purse
santur: string instrument played by striking the strings with thin curved wooden hammers
sar-afrāz: distinguished
sar'askar: commander of an army
saray: palace of the grand vizier in Istanbul
sardār: commander of the armed forces
sarkār: overseer
šarī'a: Muslim law
sarvān (*sarban* in Turkish): camel drivers
šāṭer: footman
sayis: watchmen
sepahsālār: commander of the armed forces
seğnāq (sığınak): mountain shelter
sevketlum: Majesty: title used to address the Ottoman Sultan
sheikh ul-Islam: chief religious authority of a region
siyaha: *list*
siyursatčī-başı: chief of provisions of the army

somar: measure of weight approx. 108 lbs.
sowdāgar: merchant
š'uarā (*šā'er*): poet
sundurma: open shed or awning
surahi: decanter

tabl-e bāz: a drum hung at the saddle
taḥin: flour
ta'īn: to appoint
takht: throne
takya (*tekke*): monastery
ta'līm: to instruct, to teach
tamāšā: to behold
tambur: a kind of lute, or a kind of drum
täppä (*tappe*): hill
tariqa: path
ta'ziya: passion play depicting the martyrdom of Imam Ḥosein
terkeş (*tarkeš*): quiver
tezkire: note
timin: old Turkish money
tomān: Persian monetary unit worth10,000 *dinars*
towǰi: keeper of accounts
tufenkçi: musketeers
ṭuğrā: an emperor's seal usually written in a fine ornamental script
tung (*tange*): flagon

'ušr: tax equal to one-tenth of produce

vakīl al-dowle: lord protector
vakīl (wakil, vekil): counselor, purveyor
vakīl-e ḵarǰ: purveyor
vālī: governor general, viceroy
valīne'mat: "lord of beneficence"
vazīr (*wazir, vezir*): assistant to governor, minister

waqf: religious endowments

yasak: forbidden
yedekçi: person in charge of reserve horses
yelpaz: fan
yüz-başı: head of 100 men

ẓābeṭ: revenue officer, controller
zamburak: falconets, swivel cannons
zarbāf (*zarbaft*): material woven from golden thread
ẓarrāb-kāne: mint
zencire (zanǰīr): chain
zīnat: decorate
zīyārat: to visit a scared place
zolat: gold coin worth nine *livres*
zurna: a double-reed instrument

Selected Bibliography

Abu'l-Ḥasan ibn Moḥammad Amīn Golestāne. *Majmol ot-Tavārīk*, critical edition. Tehran, 1344/1965.

Abraham Erewants'i. *Patmut'iwn paterazmats'n, 1721-1735 t'owi*. Venice [San Lazzaro], 1977.

Abraham Kretats'i. *Patmut'iwn*. Erevan, 1973 (includes the Russian translation of the *Chronicle*.

Allen, W. E. D. *A History of the Georgian People*. New York, 1932.

Anonymous. *A genuine History of Nader Cha, Present Shah…* (London, 1741).

__________. *Histoire de Thamas Kouli-Kan Sophi de Perse*. Amsterdam, 1740. 2 vols.

__________. *Relaçam de Celebre Embaxada que Principe dos Bezancudos Mandou ao Schach da Perse, Tha'mas Kouli-Khan*. Lisbon, 1744.

Aṛak'el Dawrizhets'i. *Girk' Patmut'eants* (critical edition in Russian), Moscow, 1973.

Aroutine, Tambouri (Artin Pasha). *Tahmas Quli Xanin tevariki yazilmis isdambollu Tambouri Arutinden osmanli elčisi ileyolğulugunda Ağemistan taraflarina. Bir alim Kimsenin čahdi ve hargi ile basma olundu*. Venice, 1800.

Arunova, M. R. and Ashrafian, K. Z. *Gosudarstvo Nadir-Shakha Afshara*. Moscow, 1958.

Bakīkanov, 'Abbās Qolī Āqā. *Golestān-e Erām*, critical edition. Baku, 1970.

Barsamian, Kh. *The Calendar of the Armenian Church*. New York, 1995.

Bazin, Pére Louis, S. J. *Mémoires sur les derniéres années du régne de Thamas Kouli-Kan et sa mort tragique*...vol. IV. Paris, 1780.

Birashk, A. *A Comparative Calendar of the Iranian, Muslim Lunar, and Christian Eras*. New York, 1992.

Bournoutian, G. A. *The Khanate of Erevan Under Qajar Rule, 1795-1828*. Costa Mesa, 1992.

______________. *A History of Qarabagh*. Costa Mesa, 1994.

______________. *Russia and the Armenians of Transcaucasia: A Documentary Record, 1797-1889*. Costa Mesa, 1998.

Brosset, M. F. *Collection d'Historiens Arméniens*. Vol II. St. Petersburg, 1876 (contains the French translation of Abraham Kretats'i's *Chronicle*).

__________.*Histoire de la Géorgie*. Vol. II (pts. I&II). St. Peterburg, 1856-1857.

Clairac, Louis André de la Mamye. *Histoire de Perse depuis le commencement de ce siècle*. Paris, 1750.

Durand, Sir Mortimer. *Nadir Shah*. London, 1908.

Fraser, J. *The History of Nadir Shah, formerly called Thamas Kuli Khan, the Present Emperor of Persia*. London 1742.

Hakob Shemakhetsi. *Pokhodi Takhmasp Kuli-Khana (Nadir Shakha) i izbranie ego shakhom*. Erevan, 1932.

Hakobyan, T'. Kh. *Hayastani patmakan ashkharhagrut'iwn*. Erevan, 1968.

Hammer-Purgstall, Baron J. von. *Histoire de l'Empire Ottoman*. Paris, 1835-1843. Vols. XIV-XV.

Hanway, J. *An Historical Account of the British Trade over the Caspian Sea: With a Journal of Travel from London through Russia into Persia*...London, 1753. 4 vols.

Ḥazīn, Moḥammad 'Alī. *Tārīḵ-e Aḥval*. Tehran, 1944.

Ḵʿāje 'Abd ol-Karim Maḥmud Kašmīrī. *The Memoires of Khojeh Abdul-kurreem*. Calcutta, 1788.

Kishmishev, S. O. *Pokhodi Nadir Shakha v Gerat, Kandagar, Indiiu, i sobitiia v Persii posle ego smerti*. Tiflis, 1889.

Lang, D. M. *The Last Years of the Georgian Monarchy, 1765-1832*. New York, 1967.

Lockhart, L. *Nadir Shah: A Critical Study Based Mainly Upon Contemporary Sources*. London, 1938.

_________. *The Fall of the Ṣafavī Dynasty and the Afghan Occupation of Persia*. Cambridge, 1958.

Maksoudian, K. *Chosen of God: The Election of the Catholicos of All Armenians: From the Fourth Century to the Present*. New York, 1995.

Minorsky, V. *Esquisse d'une Histoire de Nader-Chah*. Paris, 1934.

Moḥammad Mahdī Kowkabī Astarābādī, Mīrzā. *J̌ahāngošāy-e Nāderī*. Tehran, 1341/1962.

Moḥammad Kāẓem Marvī. *'Ālam-ārāy-e Nāderī*. Tehran, 1369/1990. 3 vols.

Moḥammad Kāẓem Marvī. *Nāme-ye 'ālam-ārā-ye Nāderī*. Moscow, 1960-1966. 3 vols.

_________. *Dorreh-ye Nāderi*. Bombay, 1876/1877.

Nafīsī, S. *Āḵarīn yadegār-e Nāder Šāh*. Tehran, 1300/1921.

Ormanean, M. *Azgapatum*. Constantinople and Jerusalem, 1913-1927. 3 vols.

Otter, Jean. *Voyage en Turquie et en Perse*. Paris, 1748.

P'ap'azyan, H. D. "Vagharshapat Gyughi 1725 ew 1728 t't' T'urk'akan harkats'uts'aknerê," *Banber Matenadarani* 5 (1960), 431-464.

_________. *Matenadarani Parskeren vaveragrerê*. Erevan, 1956-1968. 3 vols.

Poole, R. S. *The Coins of the Shahs of Persia; Safavis, Afghan, Efshari, Zand, and Kajars*. London, 1887.

Qodūsī, Moḥammad Ḥosein. *Nāder-nāme*. Mašhad, 1339/1960.

Simēon Erewantsi. *Dzhambr* (*Jambr*) (critical text in Russian). Moscow, 1958.

Index

‘Abbās I (Ṣafavid Shah), 32, 76
‘Abbās III (Ṣafavid Shah), 3, 18, 73
‘Abbās Qolī Khan, 73
‘Abdollāh Khan Bandarī, 73
‘Abd ol-Bāqī Khan Zangane, 111, 144
‘Abd ol-Qadīm (Mīrzā), 88
‘Abd or-Razzaq Khan, 73
‘Abd ol-Ḥasan Beg, 29, 56, 60, 63
‘Abdullah Köprülü Pasha, 3-4, 26-27, 35-40
Abovyan (district), 19, 42
Abraham II (Kat‘oghikos), 13-14
Afghans, 1
Afšār (tribe and dynasty), 2, 39, 50, 74
Aghek‘sandr (Kat‘oghikos), 14
Aghek‘sandr (Vardapet), 20, 31, 128
Aghek‘andr (Paron), 125
Aghjots‘ (Monastery), 20
Aght‘amar, 4
Aghuank‘ (Caucasian Albania), 58, 76, 107, 110, 119, 156
Aḥmad Khan, 73
Aḥmet Pasha, 63
Akhalk‘alak‘i, 45, 153
Akhaltsikhe, 39, 153
Akhurean (river), 40, 46. See also Arpa Çay.
Akhuryan, (region), 45
Akoṛi, 19
Akulis, 54, 55, 76, 106-107, 110, 124, 127, 129
Akunk, 42
Alagöz, 36
Albanians, 40-41, 160
‘Alī Akbar (Mīrzā), 88
‘Alī Mardan Khan, 73
‘Alī Mīrzā Khan, 74
‘Alī Pasha of Erevan, 22
‘Alī Pasha of Ganǰe (Ganǰ ‘Alī Pasha), 65, 81, 84, 115, 141, 144
‘Alī Qolī Beg, 114
‘Alī Qolī Khan, 16. See also Iese.

‘Alī Qolī Khan of Lār, 73
Alikuli, 103
Alinja Çay, 75
Amida (Diarbekir), 27
Anatolia, 1, 97, 158
Anna (Russian Empress), 3
Aparan (Abaran), 3, 29, 36, 103
Aq Qoyunlu, 50-51, 160
Aq Su, see New Shemakhi
Aq Täppä, 36, 42
Āqā Bāqer, 73
Aqā Beg, 87
Āqā Ḥasan, 136-137
Āqā Zamān, 114
Ara (Mt.), 36-39
Aragats (Mt.), 16, 39-40
Aṛakel of Tabrīz, 122
Ararat (Mt.), 19, 27
Ararat (Ayrarat region), 11, 19, 29, 37, 48, 55, 59, 93, 96, 126
Arax (river), 15-16, 31, 52-58, 61, 64-66, 70, 75-77, 111, 124, 139-140, 161
Ardebīl, 74, 140
Arevik, see Meghri
Aristakēs, 122
Armash, 139
Arpa Çay (river), 4, 35, 40, 43, 46. See also Akhurean.
Artashat (city and region), 55, 75, 137
Artashes I (King of Armenia), 75
Ashkhal Beg, 16, 87
Ashtarak (town and region), 16-17, 26, 29, 39, 41
Astabad, 54-55, 65, 75, 106-107, 125-136 *passim*
Astabad (monastery), 125
Astarābād, 72
Astrakhan, 57
Astuatsatur (Kat‘oghikos), 155
Astuatsatur (Paron), 64-65
Astuatsatur (Vardapet), 126
Avetaranots‘ (district), 119
Awarayr (battle), 75

Awetis (Vardapet), 21
Ayrivank' (Monastery), 20
Azerbaijan (Iranian Province), 22, 5, 55, 72, 75, 90-99, 129, 140, 144, 156, 161

Bābā Khan, 43, 46, 73, 96
Bağāvard, 38. See also Eghvard.
Baghēsh, 11, 51
Bagratids (Armenian dynasty), 49
Bagratids (Georgian dynasty), 16
Bākū, 1, 3, 74, 140
Bandar 'Abbās, 73
Bāqer Khan, 73
Bargushat, 76, 123
Barsegh, 122
Barsegh (Vardapet), 54
Bash Aparan, 29, 42
Bayazid (Bayazit), 27, 45, 51, 63-64
Behbahān, 73
Berlin (Treaty of), 27
Bitlis, see Baghēsh.
Bjni, 21
Black Sea, 11
Boghazihisar, 15
Bosnians, 40, 160
Brosset, M. F., 6, 8
Bust (village), 125
Byzantium (Rum), 32, 77, 81, 85, 111

Calcutta, 6
Canaan, 74, 140
Cappadocia, 20
Caspian Sea, 3, 76
Chanakhchi, 119
Ch'ldir (region), 45
Chavndur, 76
Chelebi (village), 50
Chorokh (river), 20
Cilicia, 4

Circassian (Cherkes), 96, 98, 144
Constantinople, 1, 14, 20, 25, 81, 97, 139, 153, 155. See also Istanbul.
Čors, 74

Daghestan, 3, 5, 57, 153
Damascus, 79
Damad Mustafa Pasha, 40. See also Saru Mustafa Pasha
Daniēl (Kat'oghikos), 27
Darashamb, 75-76, 124
Darband, 1, 3, 57, 74
Daṛoynk' (fort), 27
Dasht (village), 76, 124
Dāvūd, 130
Dawit' Beg, 2, 76, 123
Dawit' (Kat'oghikos), 27
Debed (river), 49
Delhi, 153
Diarbekir, 38. See also Amida
Dibak'lu (village), 50
Dilijan, 49
Dizak (district), 57, 59-60, 76, 107-110, 119
Dizak (village), 20
Doğubayazit, see Bayazid
Doghs (village), 30
Domboli (tribe), 73
Dovraz, 73
Dzorkegh, 120

Ebrāhīm Khan (Nāder's brother), 5, 66, 72, 78, 80, 84, 94, 104-105, 114, 126-129, 133-138
Eçek Meydān, 36
Egan (Melik), 59, 151
Eghiay (Vardapet), 54, 107-109
Eghvard (Eghward), 4, 11, 17, 34-38, 41, 65, 153
Egypt, 153
Ējmiatsin, 4, 6, 11, 13-16, 21-34, 44, 47, 50-52, 55-58, 64-66, 106-107, 124-128, 137-139, 149-151, 155-156
Ējmiatsin (city), 13
Elizavetpol', see Ganǰe

Ep'rem (Kat'oghikos), 27
Erekle II (Georgian King), 84, 153
Erevan (Erewan), 2-5, 17-29 *passim*, 35, 37, 44-52 *passim*, 59-60, 63, 71, 74, 92, 98, 103, 105, 107, 12-128, 136, 156, 158
Erinjak, 124
Erzerum, 4, 7, 45, 51, 63, 75. See also Theodosiopolis.
Esmā'īl Khan, 73
Ezr P'aṛazhnaker (Kat'oghikos), 23

France, 1
Frankanots' (village), 50

Gagh, 124
Gandzak, see Ganǰe,
Gandzasar (Monastery), 4, 58, 76, 107-110, 119, 156
Ganǰ 'Alī Pasha, see 'Alī Pasha.
Ganǰe (region), 57, 76, 107-108, 119
Ganǰe (town), 2-4, 11, 26-28, 57, 65, 111
Ganǰe (Treaty of), 3
Garin, 75. See also Erzerum.
Gaṛni, 19-20, 103
Gaspar of Boghazhizar, 15
Geghama Sea (Lake Sevan), 35-36, 42
Geghard (Monastery), 20, 42
Gegharkun, 103
Gəncə, see Ganǰe
Gēorg (Vardapet), 126
Georgia, 1-5, 28, 90, 96, 107, 114, 140, 144, 153, 159, 161
Getargel (Monastery), 20
Ghayi Ghulu (region), 45
Ghazar of P'arpi, 17
Ghazar (Paron), 17
Ghoṛch'ibek, 120
Ghorghanyan, N. K., 7-8
Ghyukas (Deacon), 55
Ghshlagh (village), 50
Gīlān, 71-72, 76, 141
Giwlmēshē (village), 123
Glakavank', 13

Goght', 53-54, 124
Golitsyn, S. D., 3, 154
Gora-dara, 42
Goris, 120-123
Greeks, 41, 160
Grigor of Shirvan, 12
Gül Aḥmet Ağa, 24
Gumush (village), 21

Hadrut, 119
Haghartsin (Monastery), 49
Haghpat (Monastery), 49, 51
Hajǰi Ḥosein, 97
Hajǰi Ḥusein Pasha, 23, 5, 51
Ḥajǰī Seif al-Din Khan Bayāt of Nišāpur, 73
Hakob (Father), 22
Hakobjan (Melik of Erevan), 16-17, 22, 26, 49, 59, 95, 103
Halidzor, 123
Hamadān, 38, 73
Hant (village), 30
Haṛants' (Monastery), 122
Harut'iwn (Vardapet), 15
Ḥasan (Imam), 90
Ḥasan 'Alī Khan, 52, 88
Hasan Jalalean (clan), 156
Havuts' T'ar (All Savior Monastery), 19
Havuz, 73
Heirat Khan, 74
Herāt, 2, 71, 93, 97, 140
Hndzuts' (Monastery), 54, 107
Ḥosein (Imam), 90
Hovhan (Vardapet), 18, 22, 26
Hovhanm (Paron), 123
Hovhannavank'(monastery), 15-16, 18, 29, 40, 127-128
Hovhannēs (Father), 15
Hovhannēs (Prior), 123
Hovhannēs of Baghēsh, 12, 14
Hrazdan (region), 21, 42
Huns, 57

Iese (Georgian King), 16
Igdir, 19
Ilkhanids 160
Imam Qolī Khan of Tiflis (David II), 74
India, 5, 74
Irits‘vanik (village), 123
Isfahan, 1, 5, 25, 73, 76, 126
Ishak Pasha, 16
Israyēl (Vardapet), 108
Istanbul, 15, 25. See also Constantinople.

J̌ahānšāh, 99
ǰa‘far (Imam), 152
J̌aqeli, 16
J̌avād, 55
Javakhēt‘ (region), 45
Jerusalem, 7, 12
J̌inli (village), 43
Julfa, 54, 76, 124, 136

Kaghzovan, 15, 45, 75
Kagizman, see Kaghzovan
Kakhet‘i, 2, 74 84, 153
Kalb ‘Alī Beg, 64
Kalb ‘Alī Khan, 74
Kalb Ḥosein Khan, 74
Kaler (village), 123
Kalushkin, I. V., 82
K‘anak‘er, 26
K‘ank‘an (canal), 30
Kap‘an (Ghap‘an, Qapān), 58, 76, 107-108
Karabagh (Qarābāğ), 2, 4, 57, 61, 76, 119, 156-157
Karačorli (Kurds), 120
Karahunj, 121
Kaṛaw (village), 123
Karbi (Karpi), 17, 26, 29, 37, 40, 103
Karchevan (village), 123
Karenis, 21

Karīm Beg, 111
Kars (river), 40
Kars, 3-4, 15, 26-29, 40, 42, 44-46, 51, 63-64, 111, 153
K'art'li, 2, 16, 84, 153
Kašān, 72, 88, 97
Kayseri (Caesarea), 20
Kazakh, 28, 74, 107, 111
Kazakh (river), 39
Kazançay, 3
Kazanchi (village), 125
Kāzrān, 73
Kecharis, 42
Kermān, 73
Kermānšāh, 73
Khach'atur (Deacon), 55
Khach'atur (Paron), 17
Khachen (district), 76, 119
Kharisimos (Paron), 64, 128, 130, 134
Khndzoresk, 120
Khor Virap, 19, 55, 75, 137
K'irashlu (village), 50
Kırk-Bulağ, 42, 103
Kirovabad, see Ganǰe
Kızılbaş, 47, 93
Ḵorāsān, 5, 18, 45, 48, 53, 66, 72, 74-75, 88, 92-93, 97, 110, 112, 115, 135, 140, 142, 158
Kör-Çavuş, 38
Ḵorramābād, 73
Kura (river), 52, 55-58, 66, 76, 139, 161
Kurdan (Treaty of), 154
Kurds, 120, 161
Kurdistan, 54, 63-64, 97

Lār, 73
Lesghians, 57, 66, 109
Loṛi, 3, 28, 74, 107, 111
Loṭf 'Alī Khan, 73

Maghakia (footman), 55, 107

Mahmud I (Ottoman Sultan), 111, 144, 152
Mākū, 744-75
Malev (village), 123
Mamikonean (clan), 13
Marand, 128
Marv, 71
Mašhad, 66, 93
Mastara (village), 50
Matenadaran (archives), 6-9, 50
Me‘yār-başı Khan, 73
Māzandarān, 72-73, 93
Mecca, 01, 152
Meghri, 53, 106, 123
Mehābād, 73
Melikjan (Kalāntar of Erevan), 29, 59, 103, 134
Melkon of Kafa (Vardapet), 126
Mesar (Monastery), 108
Mesrop Mashtots‘, 17
Mesopotamia, 74
Minorsky, V., 18
Mīrzā Abo’l-Qāsem Kāšī,
Mīrzā ‘Askar, 112
Mīrzā Kāżem, 128, 134
Mīrzā Mahdī (historian), 32, 34, 37-40, 56, 61, 88, 95, 102, 111, 150-154
Mīrzā Mo‘men, 95, 102, 111, 114
Mīrzā Rāẓī, 130, 133-134
Mīrzā Zakī, 88, 112, 114
Miwzkiwnay (monastery), 124
Mkrtich‘ (Vardapet), 54, 108
Mkrtum (Melik), 44, 59, 94, 103
Mkrtum (footman), 55
Moğān Steppe (Moqān Plain), 4-5, 52-119 *passim*, 130, 133, 139, 141, 145, 154, 161
Moḥammad ‘Alī Khan (Nāder’s son) 78, 80
Moḥammad Ḥosein Khan, 72
Moḥammad ‘Isa’ Khan, 73
Moḥammad Kāżem (historian), 38, 150, 152
Moḥammad Qolī Khan (of Erevan), 52-55, 71, 74, 84

Moḥammad Reżā Beg, 71
Moḥammad Reżā Khan, 72
Morad Tappe, 38, 41
Mortażā Qoli Mīrzā, 74, 78, 80, 84, 114
Moscow, 57, 82, 141
Moses of Khoren, 20, 53
Moṣṭafā Khan, 73
Mubarak Täppä, 42
Mughan, see Moğān.
Mughni, 17, 40
Mulla ʻAlī Akbar, 111
Mūsā Khan, 74
Mush, 13
Mustafa Pasha, 16. See also Iese.

Nāder Shah, 5, 8, 11, 16, 128, 29, 32, 36, 39, 53, 56, 59, 61, 84, 145, 153-160 *passim*
Nadr Qolī Khan, See also Nāder Shah, 2-5, 18
Nairi, 17
Nakhichevan, 2, 43, 54-55, 64, 74, 76, 98, 107, 124-136 *passim*, 156
Nariman (region), 45
Nersēs (Katʻoghikos of Aghuankʻ), 107, 110, 119, 156
New Julfa, 76
New Shemakhi, 159
Nikoghayos (Vardapet), 139
Nišāpur, 72
Noragavit, 55, 137
Norkʻ, 20

Ordubad, 53, 76
Oshakan (village), 50
Ottomans (Turks), 1-4, 35-44 *passim*, 149-155

Pʻapʻazyan, H., 6, 9
Pʻarpi, 17
Pahlavuni (clan), 21
Pʻaṛaka (village), 125
Parakar, 4, 23, 34-35
Peter the Great, 1-2

Petros (Vardapet), 125
Petros Getadardz (Kat'oghikos), 20
Pīr Moḥammad Khan, 53, 71, 93-96, 105
P'isian, 120
Pōghos, 122
Pōghos (father), 15
Pōghos (footman), 41, 55
Pulad Pasha, 38
Proshean (clan), 20

Qāǰārs (tribe and dynasty), 50-51, 74
Qandahār, 4-5, 101
Qara Qoyunlu, 50-51, 160
Qarādāğ (Karadagh), 56, 76
Qazvīn, 65, 6-73, 112
Qom, 72
Qubadli, 76
Qur'an, 90, 143

Rašt (Treaty of), 3
Ray, 73
Reżā Khan, 74
Reżā Qolī (Nāder's son), 5, 53, 78, 80, 84
Rodosto, 11

Sabirabad, see J̌avād
Sabzavār, 72
Ṣafavid (dynasty), 1-5, 27, 47, 50-53, 152, 155, 157, 160
Saghmosavank', 39
Sa'idli (district), 16
Samran, 73
Samtskhe, 16
Sanahin (monastery), 49, 51
Sardār Khan, 43, 46
Sargis, 122
Sargis (Vardapet), 20-21, 55, 107-108
Sargis of Kayseri (Vardapet), 55
Saru Mustafa Pasha, 38. See also Damad Pasha.
Sevan (lake) see Geghama

Sharur, 55, 75
Shemakhi, 3, 57, 74, 108-109, 139, 159
Shēnhēr (Monastery), 122
Shinuayr (village), 122
Shira-kala, 29
Shirakovan, 103
Shirvan, 2
Shorot‘ (Monastery), 124
Shrvēn (Melik), 123
Shuragol, 103
Silsup‘ur (tribe), 73
Šīrāz, 73
Sis, 4
Sisian, 58. See also Siwnik‘.
Siwnik‘, 53, 55
Smyrna, 7
Sobḥān Verdi Khan, 74
Ṣofiyān, 129
Soltan Ḥosein (Ṣafavid Shah), 1
Sovuḵbulāğ, 73
St. Bartholomew (Monastery), 126
St. Gayanē (church), 13, 22
St. Gregory (the Illuminator), 13-16, 19, 26, 39, 126
St. Gregory (church), 17
St. Hakob (Monastery), 19
St. Hṛipsimē (church), 13
St. John the Baptist (relics of), 12-12, 16, 67
St. Karapet (church), 15,
St. Karapet (Monastery at Erinjak), 55, 124-127
St. Karapet (Monastery in Mush), 14
St. Petersburg, 1, 6
St. Sargis (church), 16
St. Thomas the Apostle (Monastery), 124
Step‘an (Paron), 64, 129, 130, 134
Step‘anavan, 28
St. Step‘annos (church), 7
Step‘annos Ghalayji-Oğli (Vardapet), 44, 54, 102
Sublime Porte, 24, 149, 153
Surmalu, 19

Šūštar, 73
Syria, 153

Tabrīz, 2, 35-36, 65, 73-76, 94, 99, 104-105, 126-129, 133-136, 140
Tacitus, 20
T'agvoryan, H., 7
Ṭahmāsp II (Ṣafavid Shah), 1-3, 53, 73
Ṭahmāsp Khan J̌alāyer, 72, 88, 90, 114
Ṭahmāsp Qolī Khan (also referred to as the Khan, the Great Khan the Mighty Khan, Second Alexander), 2, 18, 28-29, 34, 37, 41-44, 48-5 59-70, 77-89, 139-143 See also Nāder Shah.
T'ahmaz Khan, 2, 11, 18. See also Nāder Shah
T'amar (Georgian princess), 84
T'anahat (Monastery), 122
Tandzavēr (village), 123
Taron, 11-14
Tatars, 57
T'atew (monastery), 54, 121-123
Tbilisi, see Tiflis
Tehran, 6, 65, 73, 154
T'eimuraz I (Georgian King), 74
T'eimuraz II (Georgian King), 84, 153
T'ek'irdagh, 11, 15, 21
Terek (river), 3
Ter-Hovhannēs, 7
Tghmut (river), 75, 124
Theodosiopolis, 45, 111. See also Erzerum
Thrace,11-13
Tiflis, 3-4, 16, 28, 22-48, 63, 84, 87, 140
Timur (Tamerlane), 50-51
Timur Pasha, 3, 27-28, 38
Tiwi (village), 125
Tokat, 20, 51
Tokh (village), 110, 119
Topal Osman Pasha, 3
T'ovmay (Father), 106, 110, 124, 127
T'rakia, see Thrace
Transcaucasia, 1-4, 28, 51, 153, 155
Trdat I (Armenian King), 20

Trdat III (Armenian King), 19
Trebizond, 20
Ts‘ghnay (village), 55, 124
Tsaghkunadzor (Tsaghknaydzor), 42, 103, 107
Tumanyan region, 49
Turuberan, 13

Üç-Kilisa, 13, 23, 31, 43, 47, 97, 104 See also Ējmiatsin.
Uğurlu Khan, 74
‘Umar (caliph), 90, 143
Urumiye, 73
Ushi, 16
‘Uthman (caliph), 90, 143

Vagharshapat, 6-6, 13, 21-22, 137, 139
Valīne‘mat, 18, 59, 91-119 *passim*, 126-145 *passim*. See also Nāder Shah.
Van, 3-4 38, 51
Varanda (district), 76
Vardan of Baghēsh, 12
Vardanank, 75
Vardenut (village), 29
Volynskii, A., 1
Vorotan (river), 122

Waghtang VI (Georgian King), 16, 84
Yakhni Täppä, 29
Yazd, 73

Zak‘aria of Baghēsh, 21
Zand, 50
Zangezur, 2, 58, 76, 122
Zangi Çay (Hrazdan river), 4, 21, 37

George Bournoutian is Professor of East European and Middle Eastern History at Iona College. He has taught Iranian history at UCLA and Armenian history at Columbia University, New York University, Rutgers University, Tufts University, University of Connecticut, and Ramapo College.

Other titles of interest by George Bournoutian on Armenian history from Mazda Publishers

The Khanate of Erevan under Qajar Rule, 1795-1828 (Persian Studies Series, no. 13), Center for Iranian Studies, Columbia University (New York, Bibliotheca Persica, 1992).

A History of the Armenian People, Vol. I: Pre-History to 1500 (1993; third printing, 1997).

A History of the Armenian People, Vol. II: 1500 to the Present (1994; third printing, 1998).

A History of Qarabagh: An Annotated Translation of Mirza Jamal Javanshir Qarabaghi's Tarikh-e Qarabagh (1994).

Russia and the Armenians of Transcaucasia, 1797-1889: A Documentary Record, Annotated Translation and Commentary (1998).

Also by the same author

Eastern Armenia in the Last Decades of Persian Rule, 1807-1828 (Studies in Near Eastern Culture and Society, no. 5), The G. E. von Grunebaum Center for Near Eastern Studies, University of California, Los Angeles (Malibu, Undena Publishers, 1982).